COLORADO GOLD RUSH DAYS

COLORADO
GOLD RUSH DAYS

*MEMORIES OF A CHILDHOOD
IN THE EIGHTIES AND NINETIES*

By

CARRIE HUNT BEARD

Foreword by Lowell Thomas

EXPOSITIO   NEW YORK

EXPOSITION PRESS INC., 386 Park Avenue South, New York

FIRST EDITION

DESIGNED BY AMJAD N. QURESHI

EP 42083

FOREWORD

Here is another volume for that library shelf labeled "Cripple Creek, World's Greatest Gold Camp." But it is not just another volume, a repetition of a familiar story or a rehash of history you have read. This is the drama of personal reminiscence in the high Rockies, a colorful page from America's past by one who helped to write it. This is the autobiography of Carrie Hunt Beard.

When the author speaks of the roistering days in Colorado before the turn of the century, you can believe what she says. She was there. She lived in Colorado when the Rockies were enveloped in a golden haze—the gold of Cripple Creek. She saw the boomtowns of Cripple Creek, Victor, Anaconda, Goldfield and Altman, with their miners, speculators, bartenders, dance-hall girls, prospectors and tenderfeet. She heard of the roustabouts who wandered into Cripple Creek without a dime in their britches, and who were millionaires when they left town.

But a lot more than mining went on in that supercharged, high-ozone region. Daily life went on. If prospectors came, so did families. Men arrived hoping to make a career in business, medicine, law or the pulpit. Their wives dutifully tagged along, looking for new homes where they could raise their children. This too is part of the Cripple Creek legend, a part that Carrie Hunt Beard remembers well, and describes with the feeling of an eyewitness.

If you wonder what it was like to be a little girl growing up in the Wild West when the cry was "Gold! Let's hurry and get some of it!"—turn to Chapter I and start reading.

LOWELL THOMAS

To the memory of my pioneer ancestors and all the other noble men and women who labored and sacrificed that we might enjoy the bounteous fruits of their labors. If we pause for a moment we will realize we are the pioneers of tomorrow. Our great and wonderful country is in its infancy; with the tremendous growth and achievements of such a few centuries, it is beyond our power of conception to visualize the possibilities of the future in culture, science, and general progress. Let us join the mighty chorus, and proudly sing "America the Beautiful," then bow our heads and reverently pray: "God Bless America," in progress, in power, and in lasting peace.

C. H. B.

THANK YOU

First, to God by His wonderful love toward mankind made manifest through the glorious sunshine and rain and the seasons so bountifully supplying the material needs of the world.

Then, for the loved ones and friends who make life worth living.

These things are the pure gold, not for their material value, but because they are blessings without price.

Thanks to Frances Trapp, who did my first typing and encouraged me to continue with the book.

Thanks to Mrs. A. W. Oliver of Victor, who entrusted me with the valuable newspaper clippings she had kept through the years, and for referring me to Mr. A. A. Sterns, from whom I received valuable information and inspiring letters.

Thanks, Father Kenneth Funk, for the hours you spent typing and correcting phrasing and punctuation. As an English teacher, you not only have written and published books of your own, but have ably assisted many others in completing and publishing their books.

To Lowell Thomas, who in his busy life has taken time out to write to me and encourage me.

To my cousins Charlie and Clarion Taylor for interesting stories, and last but not least to Davie Powell, my very dear friend, without whose hours and days of capable assistance in rearranging and checking data, and her most efficient typing, I am sure I could never have finished the book. She was a regular Simon Legree when it came to working on this book, and gave me no rest until it was completed.

Thanks to all for everything.

C. H. B.

CONTENTS

INTRODUCTION

My first purpose in writing a book was to record the stories my mother and grandmother told us when we were children. We never tired of listening to the experiences and escapades of their childhood, and later of the thrilling experiences in their pioneer life. Of course, the point was reached where the stories were often repeated, but they were none the less thrilling. Later, when I had children of my own, I told them the same stories and added the most interesting experiences of my own childhood. Especially thrilling was my trip in a covered wagon. "Tell us a story about the olden days" was the usual plea at bedtime. Still later, I entertained my grandchildren and great-grandchildren with the same timeworn stories. The thought occurred to me that a record of the stories in book form might be interesting to future generations, when I would not have the personal pleasure of watching the excited, interested expressions on the little faces. My little granddaughter, eight years of age, suggested that perhaps I had not told them everything, and said to think hard, and perhaps I could remember some more stories.

At first I intended to record the stories only, but as I wrote many other memories crowded in, and I started to set down later experiences, hoping they might interest others outside my immediate family. At the suggestion of my family and friends, I decided to write the book. If it is not received as enthusiastically by the public as it has been by my family, at least it will have served the purpose for which it was first intended; namely, to be a record not only of the stories I told the children, but a history of the family and what to me were the most important, authentic events of the past two generations.

At one time the title of the book was to be "The Deck," but

after careful consideration I doubted that it would attract the attention of those interested in reading western stories. "The Deck" would have a sentimental value only for those who were familiar with the true meaning of the word.

CARRIE HUNT BEARD

CHAPTER I

GRANDPAP AND GRANDMA DOLL

We were a very clannish family. My maternal grandparents, the Dolls, were born in Pennyslvania. Pap Doll was a typical Pennsylvania Dutchman, but Grandma Doll was of English descent. They left for Wisconsin immediately after their wedding in Pennsylvania, and settled in a section known as Burton, at first called Waterloo, in Grant County. The country was one vast beautiful forest, and every acre of it that was to be cultivated and planted had to be cleared and fenced.

The first houses were built of logs that were cut, dried, and the bark removed. Some were used with the bark left on, as time was important, and there was no place else for people to live. The spot Grandpap chose to make his home was ideal. The Grant River ran through part of it, and the soil was fertile and proved to be very productive.

Grandpap was not a farmer or forester. He was a cooper by trade, and here the cut trees furnished material for his work. He made all kinds of wooden containers—well buckets (everyone had at least one well), buckets for water in the house and around the barns, wooden bowls for the kitchen, butter tubs, kegs for sorghum and for elderberry wine, barrels made of light staves and hoops, for storage of fruits and vegetables, baskets, and hoops for women's dresses. (At that time women wore hoops in their dress skirts and there was a real demand for them.) These hoops were really a work of art. They were made almost entirely by hand, evenly and perfectly smoothed, then rubbed with beeswax and highly polished. Mother told us that when the young girls were coaxing to go to a spelling bee, singing bee, taffy pull, or square dance, their first thought was to polish their hoops, which had to be carefully kept so they would slide easily into the tucks made in the skirts, and splinters would not pull the fabric. Their next chore was to wash their hair and do it up in tin foil that had been carefully saved from five-pound boxes of tea, the way tea was packed at that time. She said it cut and pulled the hair, and certainly was anything but comfortable to sleep on, and of course all this was done the night before the big event.

Cousins, brothers, and other relatives followed my grandparents from Pennsylvania, and even from Germany, after Grandpap's glowing account of the wonderful country and the opportunities it offered settlers. So Burton and the immediate vicinity became a German settlement, and nearly all of the settlers were related to my grandparents.

Of course, the bright side was presented in the letters, and reports to relatives interested in coming to the new country were glowing, but the hardships of those early settlers were many. Men and women alike found every task lacked the conveniences to which they had been accustomed. At first, they did not have materials with which to work. For instance, candlelight was the only illumination; and before candles could be made, tallow had to be produced. Before wool socks could be knitted, they had to have the wool, which had to be washed and carded; and all the materials used in clothing were woven on a hand loom. Later, there was a tiny general store that sold such staples as coffee and sugar, and was also the post office; then a small church was built adjoining the cemetery.

One of the drawbacks of the pioneer country was the lack of a doctor, for of course there were illnesses and broken bones. The method of setting bones was crude, extremely painful, and most unsatisfactory. Neighbor women assisted at childbirth, very often with fatal results. No wonder pregnant women were considered both by themselves and by others as being in great danger. Antiseptics were unknown; and homemade soap was none too sterile for such use, being made of the outer fat, skin, and other fatty unusable parts of the hogs that were butchered.

The farmers butchered their hogs in the fall. That was a busy time. The hams and sides were smoked over a hickorywood fire in the little smokehouse. Then the lard was rendered, sausage made of the less tender cuts, and finally scrapple from the meat of the head. The head was cleaned, quartered, and cooked until the meat fell off the bone. This meat was then chopped quite fine and returned to the liquid in which it had been cooked. Salt and whole, hot red peppers were added, and finally, while boiling, the mixture was thickened with yellow corn meal. It had to be stirred constantly, then poured into greased square pans, and cooled. During the winter it was sliced from the pans and fried for breakfast. I still make it every Christmas for my family. It has become a tradition.

Finally the cracklings, skin, odd pieces left from the rendered lard, and all unusable fat were put into the soap barrel. Grandfather, being a cooper by trade, always had plenty of barrels around for every purpose. The lye consisted of the fine white ashes saved from the cook stove and the various other heating stoves in the house. First into the barrel went a little water, then a layer of pork leavings, then a layer of white ashes. The process was repeated until the barrel was full. In time, all the meat would be eaten by the lye and the barrel would contain soft soap, which was used for all washing purposes, including dishes. On top of the barrel was a loosely fitting wooden cover held down by a large rock. The cover was to keep inquisitive chickens from falling in or from eating the contents, which was thought to be none too good for them.

Once when Mother was three or four years old, and as broad as she was long, she dragged a box next to the barrel, climbed up, pushed the cover off, and naturally fell in head first. But she was doubly fortunate: first, the soap had not reached its most potent stage, and second, someone came out of the house, saw her feet sticking out of the barrel, and pulled her out in time. Another minute and she surely would have suffocated. Mother always ended the story this way, and we children would always add, "And then we wouldn't be here either, would we?"

Then there were epidemics, especially among the children. They had all the diseases that are common among children today, but with no wonder drugs to combat them. Whooping cough was dreaded; measles was common and often followed by fatal results; and scarlet fever took its toll. But the most dreaded was the almost always fatal diphtheria, known as black diphtheria. The little cemetery still bears witness to it today in the rows of tiny headstones. Family after family would have every child taken with the dread disease in a matter of days, and often adults contracted it with fatal results. Since all these diseases are known to be spread by germs, and the settlers were so isolated, I have often wondered just where and how the epidemics originated.

Naturally, there would be traveling salesmen, called peddlers, who came on horseback and sold thread, buttons, household wares, and clothes lines. And there was the hardware peddler, who sold nails, hammers, saws, plows, and garden tools. He visited many homes *en route* and could have been the carrier that caused suffering, death, and sorrow.

The settlers worked hard, long hours with very little equipment, and had little or no time for visiting. A funeral was an occasion that everyone took time out to attend, to dress up, and to discuss the events of the day and the many problems of the settlers. They would pack a lunch and prepare to spend the day. If the weather permitted, the food was spread on an outdoor table; but if the weather was bad, they all gathered at my grandparents' home, as it was only a short distance from the cemetery and the only large house in the settlement. They left only in time to do the farm chores.

The soil in this vast forest country was extremely fertile. Fallen leaves that had lain undisturbed for centuries had formed a leaf mold, and everything that was planted grew luxuriantly and produced grain and fruit in abundance. Nature was indeed helpful to those struggling settlers; and while the clearing of the large trees required years of hard work, the soil provided the necessities of life. At first, all the homes were built of logs; but later, when some man put in a small saw mill, the new and larger homes were built of slab siding. But only the more enterprising settlers painted them. Nearly all the painted ones were white with green trimming. The largest and best one was my grandparents' home, and it naturally became the stopping place for those passing through. An occasional preacher would stay a short time and hold services in the little church. This was really an occasion, as most of the time the services were held at my grandparents' home, and consisted of prayer meetings, reading the Bible, a prayer by the most righteous, and a short talk by one or another of the few better educated. The schoolteacher always stayed with my grandparents "for free," I am sure, as they had a large family of children attending the school.

Another ever-welcome guest, also "for free," was the peddler. Grandpap would rush out to greet him, see that his horse (they all rode horseback) was unsaddled, rubbed down, watered, and overfed. Then Grandpap would escort him into the house, show him upstairs to the guest room. This was furnished with the best homemade dresser, a large wooden bed piled high with Grand-mother's featherbed and large soft pillows made from the down of hand-plucked geese, her very prettiest hand-pieced quilts, the newest, brightest rag carpet, always the large white bowl and tall water pitcher, and the fancy towels. An extra-special meal would be prepared and served early, so that Grandpap would have a long evening to visit with the guest. His greatest delight would be to find that the peddler was a Republican or a member of any political party other than the Democratic party, as Grandpap was a radical Democrat. The argument would soon reach the "quarrel" stage and continue far into the early-morning hours. Both of them would get fighting mad, and you felt sure that the peddler would rise early and depart before break-fast, but Grandpap would be up and waiting to greet him cordially, to insist he stay a few more days; and when he finally had repacked the wares he was selling in his saddle bags, and he and his horse were rested and well fed, he would depart. Grandpap would follow him to the end of the lane, shake hands with him, and most cordially invite him to come again, all "for free," of course. And year after year he would come back, to sell and to argue.

This peddler was welcomed by all the marriageable girls of the settlement. He was called a city man, wore store clothes, and knew everything there was to know about world affairs.

One special peddler paid attention to my mother. She was a very pretty girl, and after she was married and life had become really very hard for her as the mother of a large family and the wife of a pioneer, she would remind my father that she could have married someone else and have lived in the city not too far from her home. My father resented this, and one day he told us that her great and wonderful suitor was a rope clothesline salesman. She rarely mentioned her lost opportunity after that, and never in father's presence.

There were many varieties of trees, especially large oaks. These were used for building houses (a few are still standing), furniture, barrels, barns, pens, rail fences, and the necessary firewood, as oak was used exclusively for heating and cooking. There also were many beautiful bird's-eye maples. And the many varieties of nut trees—black walnut, butternut, hazel, and hickory—furnished an abundance of wonderful food for the winter. The nuts were gathered and stored after the first heavy frost. Black walnuts and butternuts had thick outer shells and were spread on the porch or shed roofs to dry. The outer shell was removed before the nuts were stored. The hazelnuts grew in clusters, and they dried on the trees. After the first heavy frost, the burs would pop open, and the first strong wind would scatter them under the trees so that they were easy to gather. The hickory nuts were much the same, and easily gathered. The wood of the black walnut trees was used later to make our valuable furniture, which is so rare and coveted today.

There were a few slippery elm trees. The part of the bark that was used for medical purposes grew between the tree trunk proper and the outer bark, and it is all the name implies—slippery. As youngsters we would peel the bark back, cut strips of it, and eat it—slick and almost tasteless. I do not remember any good or bad results. I think the pioneers also used it as a poultice, and at least it must have been very soothing. Then there was the sassafras tree. Its bark was used for tea—especially in the spring—along with treacle (molasses) and sulphur, and was a regular spring medication supposed to thin the blood and guard against contagious diseases. There were also some sugar maples for maple syrup and sugar candy, and apple and crab-apple trees. Wild pulm and cherry trees were scattered through the woods and are still plentiful today. A few years ago when I visited my cousin, we drove through the woods back of their farm home and gathered several varieties of beautiful apples. They were perfect, and free from worms. I was told that the birds carried the seeds, and that they were free from worms because of the oak trees that grew around them. Wild berries were plentiful, as were the elderberries and grapes for the kegs of wine and stores of winter jelly. The rail fences were covered with luscious blackberries. Mother said the May apples, which grew on small bushes in profusion and bore fruit during the month of May (and regularly made the children nauseous, as they were sickening sweet), were not used for canning or for the table but made delicious sauce and pies. There was also a small bitter apple that, when raw, puckered the mouth like our choke cherries.

Mushrooms grew in season. There may have been several varieties, but I remember just one, and at the time did not know what it was. One day in the spring as I was on my way home from school with my cousins, I saw what I at first thought was a kind of flower growing by a fallen tree. It was about eight or nine inches tall, sort of cone-shaped, and the outside looked exactly like tripe. Close to it were several more, and we filled our dinner pails with them. Aunt Mary Jane knew at first glance that they were rare mushrooms. She knew just how to prepare and cook them in sweet butter. They were delicious.

We ("Mandy's children," everyone called us back there) both feared and loved Aunt Mary Jane, mother's oldest sister, more than anyone else in the large clan. We soon learned that her bark was worse than her bite. And I guess it would have to be, she spent all her waking hours talking steadily, mostly scolding. Her poor husband, Uncle Frank, used to say, "Jaw, jaw, jaw from morning till night! Don't your jaws ever get tired?"

Actually she was energy personified. I never saw her when she wasn't working. She just kept on scolding to sort of keep

time with whatever she was doing. And for all the outlandish
things she said, we knew she had the proverbial heart of gold.
She was a wonderful cook and loved to prepare the food her
guest liked best. Whenever we could manage a visit to her
house, it was difficult to get away. She would set off in a
perfect fury of work, preparing a feast of the dishes we liked
best, and simply laying us out all the while. Once she said we
were "lazy hogs" who never thought of anything but our bellies.
She seemed to enjoy scolding us as much as she enjoyed
watching us eat her wonderful food. She always reminded me
of Pap Doll arguing violently with his traveling salesmen. Only
no one could really argue with Aunt Mary Jane; you just
couldn't get a word in edgewise.

Her husband, Uncle Frank, was a small dark man who
seldom had a word to say, which was probably just as well.
But we children held him in awe. His little black eyes seemed
to send out sparks of fire whenever he snapped out a few curt
words. They had three children of their own, Joe, Gilbert, and
Allie. Later, like all the families of that time, they adopted a
little girl, Bert, from the county farm. And again, much later,
three baby girls were born to them, one after the other. Aunt
Mary Jane was passionately fond of each of them. She kept them
spotlessly clean, really looking like little wax dolls. She hovered
over each one in turn like a mother bird watching over her
babies. But each one lived only a few short weeks. And try as
she might, Aunt Mary Jane could never conceal the terrible
sorrow she felt at each of these successive tragedies.

While they were a hard-working family, they never seemed
to do well. Their farm was run down, the house was poorly
furnished, and decidedly poorly heated. I have reasons to know
about that. One of Aunt Mary Jane's pet hates was to have the
children get out of bed after they had climbed the rickety
stairs to the one big room overhead and crept into the big bed.
She always warned each of us individually as we went up, that
we were not to get out of bed. The room had five double beds
and no rugs. We could see the light burning downstairs through
the cracks in the floor, and by leaning out from the bed I could

see her and Uncle Frank hovering over the frail little baby they were trying so desperately to keep alive.

It was bitterly cold upstairs, but the horrible threats that hung over us always made it imperative for one or the other of us to try getting up. We would slip out of bed with the utmost caution, never daring even to think of shoes. But every board in that floor, at the slightest pressure, would squeak like a soul in anguish so at the first move she always heard us, and the storm would break. She would start out on the youngest.

"Is that you, Bert?"

Naturally, there was no answer, even if it happened to be Bert who was up.

"Is that you, Allie?"

And so on up the line, until finally she reached poor Joe, the oldest. Joe was quiet, like his father, and never dared to get up, and I am sure his mother knew it. But by the time she got to him she had worked herself into such a fury that she couldn't have stopped if she wanted to. Besides, there was no one left to blame, as she never went down the line again.

"Joe, you big sight, is that you?" We always waited for that line, and it always started us giggling. Then the fireworks would really start. We knew perfectly well that she had never struck anyone in her life; but by the time she got going good, we couldn't feel too sure she wouldn't. Oh, how that woman could scold!

One morning I shall never forget. I didn't think it could be possible, but that morning there was even more bustle than usual. Uncle Frank and Joe were trying to load Aunt Mary Jane's fat hog into the wagon to take it to market. She had fed it since it was a little pig, and now it was huge. I had never seen such a fat pig in my life, and I don't think I ever have since. It was really an engineering problem to get that hog into the wagon. And to complicate matters, Aunt Mary Jane was busily rehearsing the long list of things she wanted for the house and family with the money from the sale of the hog. But finally the hog was loaded and they drove away to Potasi, six miles distant.

They couldn't have been gone more than ten minutes when they drove back into the yard. Evidently the excitement and exertion had been too much for the grossly overweight animal. When Uncle Frank turned to see how the pig was doing in the back of the wagon, it was lying motionless on the floor. There was only one thing to do. He cut her throat to bleed her, and turned back to face the cyclone. We younger children couldn't understand what all the "jawing" was about over a simple butchering. I recall thinking that Uncle Frank must have become quite deaf, after I had asked him three times for the sweetbreads and got no answer. Finally he said, "Hogs don't have sweetbreads."

That was a day! And for several days afterward there was much to do—bacon and hams to cure and smoke, sausage to make, lard to render, scrapple to take care of—but not for a moment was the tiny baby neglected.

One summer when Mother took us to visit our grandparents and relatives in Wisconsin, Grandpap hired us to hoe the sweet corn. The pay was twenty-five cents to spend at the Fourth of July celebration held at Beetown, a wide place in the road about twelve miles distant. My brother Gil and I, who were six and eight years of age respectively, and our four cousins who lived on adjoining farms, considered the pay very generous. We all had hoes and worked like beavers at first, but the sun was very hot and the rows long. At first, we each took a row and did a pretty thorough job. We worked only mornings, as Mother thought the afternoons were too hot. Besides, we were really tired. After a few days, either the weeds got taller and tougher or we were more tired, so we decided that hoeing every other row would do just as well. Grandpap inspected the job every day and at first "bragged on us," but I saw him put his hand over his white beard, and I am sure it was to hide a smile. At any rate, he paid us, and twenty-five cents bought quite a lot of good ice cream at the celebration.

While there was an abundance of wild game—deer, wild geese, and turkeys—to supply the table with a variety of meat, I doubt that there were any buffalo. But Grandpap had a wonderful buffalo robe. I think he either bought it or traded with some salesman for it. He kept it in the front bedroom, and on rare occasions some favored guest was allowed to use it as a lap robe in the cutter on very cold days.

Bears were numerous, and Mother told us that the children would cover their heads in the night when panthers screamed. The sound was like that of a woman in distress.

We children used to beg her to tell us about the time the gray wolves followed them from school. Some farmers had spotted a pack of gray wolves, the kind that attacks humans. They had lost young lambs and other young animals and were planning to form a hunting party, and shoot them, but the hunt had to wait until after the harvest. One of the farmers would meet the children after school to take them to their homes. They warned the children about the wolf danger, and told them to wait for someone to pick them up. Although it was several miles to the little schoolhouse, they walked by themselves in the morning, as wolves rarely attack in the early part of the day; but they were told what to do if they should see any wolves. They must never run, as the wolves would also run, and could run faster than they could.

One night the farmer escort was later than usual, and the children started for home without him. They had gone only a short distance when someone saw wolves following off to one side. Of course they were dreadfully frightened, but remembered what they had been told. They walked but did not run. Mother was the youngest, she was in her first year at school, and quite chubby. Her little fat legs were so short that she couldn't keep up. She trailed behind, crying bitterly. It was really a welcome sight when two farmers with shotguns showed up in a wagon. Every time Mother told the tale we would hold our breath and hope the wolves wouldn't catch them, and we always asked, "Did they catch you?"

Her answer always was the same: "If they had, you wouldn't be here."

As a young woman, Mother was slender and beautiful, and I am including her wedding picture in this book so that you can see for yourself. As a child, however, she had been a fat little girl, very short and almost completely round. One day she crawled under the barn after a swallow's nest that she knew was far back in the darkness. As she crept through the dust underneath the barn, the floor got closer and closer to her fat little bottom, but finally she reached the nest, and sure enough, there were four baby birds in it. Crawling in had been bad enough, but wriggling out backward, with the nest of little birds, was impossible. The nails from the floor caught her dress, and soon she was wedged tightly, far back under the barn. The little birds were covered with lice, which crawled up her arms and over her face and into her hair, and for a while she was a very miserable little girl. At last someone heard her cries, removed a board from the barn floor, and got her out. When Mother would tell us this story, we children would always ask her what happened to the birds; but she could not remember just what she did with them.

Then she would tell us about the big tomcat that insisted on sleeping right in the middle of the white bedspread on Grandmother's bed. The girls had to do all the washing, and it wasn't easy to wash in those days. The water had to be pumped from the outside well, and carried in buckets to the boiler on the kitchen stove to be heated, then carried outside again, after the washing, to be emptied. All in all, the girls decided that the cat just wasn't worth the extra washing he caused them. So one day when Grandmother was gone, they got a burlap sack, inserted the cat and a large rock, tied it up securely, and dropped it off the nearby suspension foot bridge that crossed the Grant River. When Grandmother returned, she noticed their guilty looks, and soon accused them of doing away with the cat, for they had threatened to do just that during many a washing. Mother and her sisters confessed, but insisted that they were not sorry. And it was just as well. That evening when the boys came from the barn with their pails of milk, the cat was calmly sitting on the back steps, waiting for his share.

While she was at this age Mother had a habit of running away. This was most annoying, since farms were far apart and there were no telephones, so someone would have to stop work to hunt for her. Finally she had an experience that stopped her from wandering. One fine winter day she ran away to a neighboring farmhouse, where the wife was doing her Saturday baking. She had pumpkin, custard, and apple pies cooling on the kitchen table, directly under an upstairs open register. In those days there were no stoves on the second floor, which was heated by cutting out sections of the floor and the ceiling beneath to allow the heat from below to come up. Mother had gone upstairs and was playing with the children of the house in the bedroom over the kitchen, when she decided to look down through the opening in the floor and see what was going on downstairs. With her usual penchant for losing her balance, she immediately went hurtling through the air and landed right in the midst of all the pies. It was really quite a fall, and she was painfully bruised, frightened, and a total mess. And so were the pies. Naturally the cook was upset too, what with all her pies ruined and the kitchen to clean. So as soon as she had extricated Mother from the cookery, she sent her home in no uncertain manner, being careful to warn her against future visits. Mother claims that she never ran away again. At least she didn't go to that house.

Snakes were numerous, and although most were harmless, some were very poisonous. The rattler was the most common of the poisonous type, and there were few known antidotes to rattlesnake venom. If a person or animal was unluckily bitten by one, suffering and death often followed. Black snakes were very common and very large at maturity. They protected themselves by whipping around when attacked by humans or animals. Mother said she had seen them as large around as a stove pipe, and very long, they certainly looked formidable. They were very fond of young chickens, and once when I was at Aunt Mary Jane's, we heard a strange noise and commotion out near the barn, and saw a flock of small chickens around a huge black snake. My aunt said the snake had charmed them (perhaps they were curious), and when they were close enough, the snake easily picked up as many as it could devour. But Aunt Mary Jane soon put an end to it with a hoe, and hung it over the clothes line, where it writhed after she said it was dead, and would continue to show life until after sundown, according to tradition.

Of course, snakes must have gotten into the houses at times, but I remember hearing of only one such instance. Grandmother related that once a snake kept sticking its head up through a knothole in the floor, and she ran for one of the men to kill it. But when they returned no head showed up, so a plug was put in the hole. But at suppertime, when she went to the bread box, which had been left slightly ajar, there coiled around the loaves of bread was Mr. Snake!

Grandpap had a row of hives at the end of the garden, and he handled the bees with ease. They never stung him. When they would swarm and a new hive formed, there was a lot of action, and the din made by the pounding of tin pans and pails to attract and capture the queen bee was really exciting.

One day when Grandpap was driving to near-by Potasi, he heard someone say hello. He stopped his team and looked around, expecting to see a friend or neighbor beside the road. There was no one in sight, so he drove on, rather puzzled. Then the same voice said hello again, but there was still no one in sight. And when he heard someone say, "Where you going?" it made him mad. He thought it was someone hiding behind the rail fence that ran along the road. So he answered, "None of your business." Just then he saw a black crow sitting on the fence. Someone's pet crow had escaped and was having fun with Grandpap.

The last time Mother took the four youngest children to visit, I was eleven years of age. I remember waiting for the train at the depot in Colorado Springs. My father slipped me a dime, a lot of money at that time.

"When you are looking out the train window and the telegraph poles go clicking by," he said, "think of your daddy at home alone. I will miss you."

We were returning for a momentous occasion—my grandparents' golden wedding anniversary—and the clan from near and far was invited. Mighty were the preparations. A cousin of Mother's who was considered the best cook around came to help

prepare the banquet. I can still see the huge cakes, every kind
of pie, fried chicken, baked hams, in fact, just everything available to make the feast complete, and the gifts were displayed in
the parlor, a room we seldom were permitted to enter.

It had a very special carpet on the floor, not a rag one, as
was common in most homes, but a store rug. There was a shiny
horsehair couch and chairs, and a most unusual prized piece of
furniture—a piano—that had been bought with money saved
from the sale of eggs and Grandmother's hand-made articles. It
represented years of labor. She had given it to her youngest son,
Charlie, who had gone to a near-by small town and taken les-
sons, and could play in her estimation "just beautifully." The
walls were hung with large framed pictures of the family—
Grandmother's and Grandpap's in the most conspicuous places.
But one picture was lacking, that of the oldest son, Jones. When
I asked Mother about it, she said, "Don't ever say a word about
it, and someday I will tell you."

At that time there was a popular song, "There's a Name
That's Never Spoken and a Mother's Heart That's Broken, and
a Picture With Its Face Turned Toward the Wall." There was
no picture hung in the space where it had been, and neither
Uncle Jones nor any of his family was at the golden wedding.

This is what Mother later told me: Grandpap loved fine
horses, and he always had a matched team of carriage horses
that he and he alone drove hitched to a fancy light-top buggy
on his occasional trips to near-by towns. Fine horses were his
hobby; he raised them and sold them for what at that time were
fabulous prices.

When he decided to make a day's trip to town, generally
Potasi, a very small village about six miles distant, everyone was
kept busy the day before. The harness had to be greased and the
buckles polished and the buggy washed; and early the next
morning the horses were brushed and curried until their slick
coats fairly shone. He would appear in his Sunday best, a white
shirt, bright tie, and a tall hat. Every hair in his long white
beard was in place. He carried a long whip, but I doubt that he
ever used it. It was mostly for effect.

Grandmother smoked a little clay pipe, and generally that was his excuse for the trip—to buy her smoking tobacco, or perhaps some coffee or sugar. But the main reason was a day's outing, in style, and to spend several hours in the general store where he would gather all the juicy bits of gossip, and, if he was especially lucky, find someone to argue with on his favorite subject—politics. He had one very fine young mare; she was not saddle broken, but he had put a bridle on her and trained her to be guided by a bit.

One Saturday Grandpap departed on his usual trip to town. He had warned the boys never to take one of his prize horses out for any purpose. That day Jones was plowing corn across the Grant River. He came into the house very suddenly—he was very white. He got the big shotgun and hurried out without a word. Grandmother heard a shot and soon he came back. He went upstairs and came down with a small bundle of his clothes, kissed his mother, and left.

Jones had hitched the fine mare to the plow. She became frightened and had run away, and the plow blade had severed her hind leg. It was many years before they heard from him. Finally the urge to return to his boyhood home became so strong that he returned with his family, and settled several miles away. He saw his brothers and sisters and their families, but he never came home again. Grandpap never forgave him.

It will probably seem strange to people in this modern world, but we all loved Grandpap for all his gruff ways. He was German, born and raised in Pennsylvania, and had every right to be a stubborn Dutchman. I always felt that he wanted more than anything else to forgive Jones, but he just didn't know how. Being stubborn was just part of his moral code; and remaining estranged from his eldest son, in Grandpap Doll, had something of an Old Testament quality, like Abraham ready to sacrifice Isaac.

Another couple living in Burton celebrated their golden wedding anniversary while we were still there, and of course everyone was invited; but Mother decided four children were too many to take. So she and Grandmother, with the two young-

est, drove to the party in the two-seated light buggy, leaving
Gil and me protesting loudly at being left at home. But Grandfather came to the rescue. As soon as Mother and Grandmother
were out of sight, he told us to get dressed in our Sunday best;
and shortly the three of us were on our way to the festivities.
Needless to say, Mother was none too pleased when we arrived,
but there was nothing she could do, as no one, but no one, ever
won an argument with Grandpap.

My younger brother Gil and I usually made the rounds
together, visiting all the relatives. On our last visit we stayed
until after Thanksgiving, and we would walk several miles each
day to the little country school, with our cousins. Each day was
like a picnic, with our wonderful lunches. I know now they were
really special on our account, but at any time they were a
healthy, hardy bunch, and must have been well fed. We had a
wonderful week at Uncle Jones and Aunt Alice's. Then we
spent a week with Uncle Henry and Aunt Minnie and my three
cousins. Matie May was three days younger than I, and we said
we were twins. It was fun there, too, and I decided to stay all
winter and go to school with them. Aunt Minnie was not well,
however, so Mother decided against it. When the new baby
girl arrived, they wrote that they had named her Carrie for me.
This pleased me no end, as I didn't think my name was pretty,
and thought they must like me very much.

Each place we visited offered at least one outstanding event,
and a ram was the big one at Uncle Henry's. The farmhouse was
built at the foot of a wooded hill, and there was a swing on a tree
about halfway up the hill. Matie May and I went up for a swing.
We were both standing up facing each other on the swing board,
and had worked up a good high speed, when she suddenly
jumped off. She half fell, but made for the fence fast. I didn't
know what it was all about until I saw Mr. Ram, head down,
making for the swing. I was a little late, but I followed her style,
and departed. Luckily for me I had enough presence of mind to
give that swing board a good fling, and the ram struck it first
before he took after me. I ran and fell just before I reached the
fence, but managed to roll under just in time, before the ram

caught up with me. He came head on against the fence with full force, and there was a loud bang. If he had butted me that hard, he would have knocked me "into the middle of next week," as Father used to say. Matie May was convulsed with laughter, and when I recovered from my fright, I joined in with her. It was funny then, but it could have been a tragedy.

There were several distant settlements. One was called Dutch Hollow, where most of the settlers were Dutch immigrants—a very industrious group. They were known for their tendency to put the cart before the horse, as the saying goes. And Father often told the story about the Dutchman telling about the fox: "The fox ran the hill up, the fence over, and the haystack under."

There was also a small settlement called North Andover. Most of these people were Irish, among them my Uncle Charlie, who married my Aunt Della. While there were minor disagreements between the different settlements, as a whole they were industrious, friendly, and peace-loving people.

About fifty-five years later, my younger son, John, and I visited the many places mentioned in the stories I had told him in his childhood. By then all of my mother's and father's relatives were gone, with the exception of my cousin Otho and his wife, who still lived on the farm, and cousin Gene and his wife, who were living in Lancaster, a fairly good-sized town made up mostly of retired farmers. My dream of showing John the beloved scenes of my childhood was rudely shattered, because where once had stood my grandfather's large frame farmhouse and big barns, not a stick remained. For the Grant River, which had never been known to reach flood stage, had gone on a rampage and washed everything away—even the suspension bridge from which Father had had his first glimpse of Mother. In the little town of Burton there remained only two or three houses. And the general store, which also housed the post office once operated by my grandpap, was closed. However, one familiar landmark was still intact—the little church adjoining the cemetery where most of the relatives I remembered were buried.

I was surprised to see how well it was kept up. The headstones were in place and upright, and the grass, most of it short, was very green—evidence that someone remembered and cared. A few graves were overgrown with weeds, and those weeds were very tall, mostly thistles. Since it was early fall, they were in bloom, a soft shade of lavender, and the plant itself, a pale green, looked as if it might recently have been lightly powdered. They were really beautiful. As we wandered about reading the names on the many stones, we came to one that was more recent and had no grass on it; but right in the middle of it was the tallest, loveliest thistle imaginable. It was fully six feet tall and in full bloom. The name on the stone was not familiar to me, and as we stood there amazed at the height and beauty of the huge weed, my cousin said, "This sure beats all. That man carried the mail many years up until the time of his death. He was an old man, and lived alone in a tiny house after the death of his wife; and weeds, especially thistles, grew so rank and so tall that you could not find the few flat stones that had been a walk, and could scarcely reach the back door. The front door was almost hidden. And he has brought the finest one here for company."

Although I was disappointed to see the many changes nature had wrought in the landscape of my childhood, we enjoyed our trip very much. It was the fall of the year, and the woods, with the oak trees in their vivid colors of red and gold, were breathtakingly beautiful. We gathered several varieties of apples from the trees that grew in the woods, and in spite of further disappointments, when visiting other localities, we really had a wonderful time. We left with our car loaded with fruit and vegetables, and also carried away the memory of many happy hours spent with our few remaining relatives.

CHAPTER II

"BRIDDISH HOLLOW"

My paternal grandparents, the Hunts, were not like the Dolls. They were not farmers but tradespeople, and why they ever came to the wilds of Wisconsin I do not understand. The only business that might have come close to paying was a general store, but there was no store. They thought it was too near Potasi, about four miles distant, where there was a fair-sized store, and where one could occasionally buy a several-days-old newspaper. In it was a little nook for a post office, where one rarely received a letter. Of all things, Grandfather had a little meat market. One of his seven trades was that of a butcher. They must have had an ice house where in winter they stored ice cut out of the Mississippi River, but the farmers all butchered their own meat. The only industry was mining; there were some small mines near by. I am not sure whether it was zinc or lead they produced, but the few miners lived in "Briddish"; and, since they were itinerants, Grandmother conducted a small boarding-house. Thus they managed to eke out an existence, and out of eight children, five lived to a fairly good old age.

The Hunts were very different from Mother's people. Games, especially card games, were always evident and enjoyed by all, that is, until the time when Grandfather questioned a play made by Grandmother. It made her very angry that anyone should doubt her integrity in a card game, and she threw her cards down and said she would never play again. And to my knowledge she never touched a card again as long as she lived, although she enjoyed watching other people play.

They made wine and drank and served it, but were very temperate. I doubt if they were ever intoxicated. Grandmother had been used to ale in England and enjoyed a glass of beer, which they very rarely were able to buy, except perhaps when

someone went down the Mississippi to Dubuque, Iowa, on a rare
business trip, and brought back a bottle or two as a surprise
gift, usually for Grandmother.

Most of the early settlers of the section must have been
immigrants, as the names of the little settlements signify. There
was Waterloo (Burton), British ("Briddish") Hollow, North Andover, and Dutcher Hollow. The children from Dutch Hollow
attended the British Hollow School; and while the German
children were taught English, the English children also learned
to speak German. My father spoke German fluently. The teachers were generally men, and they believed in the pupils' learning
the hard way, and did not spare the rod. Father said the bad
part of the whippings was that the child was sent out to cut the
hickory switches to be used. If he came back with too few or
too small ones, the ones he brought first were added to the
second or even third collection, until the teacher considered
them sufficient, and the beatings were severe. And to add to
the punishment, if the pupil told about it at home, and his
parents considered he had deserved it, he got another one for
good measure. I asked my father if the children were very bad
and deserved such treatment. He said no, they were not bad
youngsters, and were very much in awe of the teacher, but they
were slow to learn in a room full of different grades and were
taught "readin' and writin' and 'rithmetic to the tune of the
hickory stick."

While most of the time the teacher was upheld in his decisions, there was one who went a little too far. One young girl,
sixteen years of age, was a slow pupil, since she hadn't been
allowed to go to school regularly, having had to help in the
house and field. She must have felt self-conscious, being so much
larger and older than the others. One day she rebelled, and the
teacher promptly took her across his knee, the long dress and
petticoats came up, and he gave her a severe spanking. The
community felt he had gone too far, and at a public meeting he
was sent down the road. The girl was so humiliated she never
went back to school.

The most outstanding person I have known in my life was

Grandmother Hunt. She was a most remarkable person, respected and beloved in her home and by everyone, not only in her immediate community, but for miles around. She was known as "Ma" Hunt. She was the youngest of a large family, and the best beloved of her father, a country squire in Somersetshire, England. She was reared a lady, and said all that was required of such a young lady was to make her own bed properly and sew a fine seam. When she fell in love with a young man who was a tradesman (he not only was a tradesman, but master of seven trades), her father was furious. He felt she not only had degraded herself but had disgraced the family.

Her name was Mary Ann Pain, and her father found her a match for his pride and stubbornness. But she was twenty-one, and could and did make her own decisions. In his household his word was law. To oppose him meant exile, but she was governed by her own good judgment and the dictates of her heart. The young couple made their plans. The lure of the new world was in their blood, and everywhere the reports of opportunities in the United States offered to capable young men were being talked about. Friends wrote and encouraged them to come. If they remained in England and were married, there was no hope they would be tolerated in her father's home. So they carried out their plans. A ship was sailing on a certain date. Her mother, while she did not come out openly and approve, helped with the wedding arrangements at the Episcopal church, and the packing of gifts. Her father told her she would have no share in the inheritance, but her mother had some money, and assured her she would share and share alike with her brothers and sisters. As far as the inheritance was concerned, however, she was not in the least interested; but she was the youngest and closest to the heart of her proud father, and for many years had been chosen to tie his kerchief about his neck before he left for his survey of his estate. That last morning was no exception, and he said, "For the last time, lass." He did not attend the wedding, and she never saw him again. In fact, she never saw any of her people again, but she exchanged letters with all the other members of her family regularly. I doubt that she ever mentioned one hardship or sorrow she endured in her new life.

The estate must have been quite large, as she mentioned the gamekeeper and how they aways had wild birds. She said they hung the meat until it ripened, and I guess that is just the right word. Birds were hung with feathers on, and not dressed until they were to be roasted and served. Among the things she brought with her was a wall clock that struck the hour and a set of blue dishes. I still have the clock and one dinner plate, and my son Earl has the sampler she made with two alphabets embroidered on it, one in printed letters, the other in script, the numbers up to ten, and her name.

All little girls in her class made samplers. They were made on linen cloth with a mesh, so that the little cross-stitches would be uniform. And the sampler was displayed proudly, especially if it was perfect; and perfect it was supposed to be when finished.

I once asked Grandmother if she ever had moments, when the going got rough, when she regretted her decision. She said, "No, never once." But she wished she had never been born when she was seasick for thirteen weeks on the small sailing vessel that rose and fell with every swell across the Atlantic Ocean. While New York was different from London and Liverpool and other large cities she had visited in England, it was not really more than she had expected. There were no Flatiron Buildings or other skyscrapers then, but there was decidedly more hustle and bustle, and an air of excitement. They took a room in a boardinghouse, and Grandfather went to work at one of his trades, that of tailor, until they could decide just where to go, as they had no intention of staying in New York. She said the landlady was very kind and understanding, and when she rubbed blisters on her knuckles washing a few clothes, the landlady took over and told her she should rub the clothes and not her fingers. When she wandered down to the markets, she was intrigued by the large red fruit she saw—then called love apples, now tomatoes. She had never seen tomatoes before, and bought some, but she said they didn't like them.

Meanwhile, they saved every cent possible that winter, and listened to everyone who talked about the wonderful West, and the places young men were planning to go to make their fortunes. The Germans were interested in Pennsylvania, and most of them decided that that was the best place. The English favored Ohio. Then my grandparents met a couple who had heard from some of their people in Wisconsin. They gave such glowing reports of it that they decided to go there.

Since my grandparents were expecting their first baby in the early summer, they made plans to leave New York in the fall. After the baby girl, Matilda, was born and a few weeks old, they set out in a light wagon with one horse hitched to it, and all their belongings packed in the back. They were headed for Wisconsin and the real beginning of an eventful life.

It was a long trip, especially for the tiny baby, but she was strong and healthy and stood the trip fine.

The main reason they chose that part of Wisconsin was because of the mines. They were lead and zinc mines, and since farming was not one of Grandfather's trades, he had a shop or store in mind. And since miners had to have a place to stay and eat, Grandmother fitted into the picture as a boarding-house keeper, something she certainly knew nothing about, but was determined to learn. She had never cooked a meal in her life. Of course, there were failures at first, but eventually her home-made bread and pies excelled those baked by her kindly neighbors, who taught her the art. She said one of the things that bothered her most was the lack of screens on doors and windows, and she fought flies and flying insects constantly during the warm months.

The family, while it existed, did not prosper as they had hoped; but it did increase. Although epidemics took several infants and small children, they had three grown daughters and two sons when they later left Wisconsin for Kansas.

With all her busy home life, Grandmother always had time to help any neighbor in distress, and she was known far and wide as a most capable midwife. It was never too hot or too cold or the snow too deep to deter her, when called upon to deliver one of the many babies born in the wilderness, and she always had a supply of simple remedies to pack in her basket. There were the dried watermelon seeds to steep and make a tea for the new mother, and dried catnip and peppermint leaves for the colicky baby.

Doctors? There were none for many miles. Dubuque, Iowa, was perhaps the nearest place, and much could happen before it was reached and a doctor could make the return trip. A doctor's certificate of death or birth was unknown; and the settlers made their own rough coffins for burying their dead. Grandmother Hunt was the one called to lay out the dead, bathe them, put pennies on their eyes to hold the lids closed, and finally dress them for the last time.

Many wonderful women lived and struggled in the early days of our country, but I feel sure they had been accustomed to more hardships and had more early training than she. That is why to me she was so outstanding and wonderful.

In spite of their industry and hardships, Briddish Hollow had not come up to their hopes and expectations, and held no promise for the future. So because of their disappointments and Grandfather Hunt's failing health, at this time they were considering a move; and Father's choice of a new location was instrumental in their decision to follow him to Kansas.

CHAPTER III

KANSAS

Father told me about the first time he saw Mother. His family was English and so was Grandmother Doll. On his days off, he used to walk over to the farm to be with the Doll boys and Grandmother, whom he considered to be English like himself. One day as he approached the Grant River, he saw a girl standing on the suspension foot bridge, but when he got there she had disappeared. He knew she couldn't have gone far, so he stood on the bridge and looked for her on the bank. Suddenly he had an inspiration, and called out, "You might as well come out; I know you're there."

So Mother came out from behind one of the bushes that lined the river bank, trying to keep her feet covered with her dress, for she was barefooted. That was why she had hidden when she saw Father coming. Anyway, they walked up to the farmhouse together, and from that time on it was taken for granted all around that they would eventually be married; but until they were, Mother's older sister, Aunt Alice, was always with them. Father never even kissed Mother until after they were married, although they did hold hands now and then. Once I asked my father when he had a chance to propose to Mother. He thought for some time before he answered, then he said, "I don't think I ever did. Your mother and I and everyone in both families just took it for granted."

But what seemed most strange to me was that he never even knew she existed until he met her by the bridge, although he had been coming to visit her brothers for years. I'm sure that he had always known that Aunt Alice was around.

When my father and mother were married, Mother was eighteen, Father twenty. The wedding was at her home in Burton. They came to Briddish Hollow and stayed overnight at his home. He had saved and bought a light wagon and a horse, and his belongings and their gifts were packed in the back of the wagon. Her wedding gifts consisted of lovely handmade and hand-quilted bedspreads, two down pillows, and a wonderful featherbed made from the finest goose down and the smallest feathers plucked from her mother's flock of geese, handmade and embroidered linens trimmed with fine crocheted lace, a small set of dishes, cooking utensils, and a small rocking chair Grandpap had made by hand, in which to rock the future babies.

Mother's eighteenth birthday was September 5, which was also her wedding day. Since it was early fall, the young chickens were just right for frying, so they were included in the large lunch box that was packed with enough food to last several days on the trip to Kansas. Some had to be given to the hospitable settlers or exchanged for milk and butter, as they had no means of keeping either from spoiling along the way. They were welcomed by the settlers as overnight guests and urged to stop and rest a few days, especially to visit, as guests were few and far between.

They were interested in the reports Father gave them of the new country and their destination, one of the small towns near Topeka. These pioneer settlers considered themselves 'way out West. Kansas was certainly the jumping-off place, and still inhabited by hostile Indians and buffalo. Mother said that after a few nights listening to their horror tales, she begged to go back home and settle there; but she didn't know how determined her husband could be. She found out then and later in life that when he set his mind on anything, that was it. And so in fear and trembling she rode along close to his side, while he told her about the big cities she would see—Kansas City and the next larger one, Topeka, near which he had decided to settle. He told her about the railroad, its freight and passenger cars, and the big steam engine that pulled them, the coal mines and all the advantages, and tried to convince her it wasn't as bad as they had pictured it. And of course the settlers' stories were exaggerated; but it was bad enough, and she said she was afraid and homesick, and often begged to return to Wisconsin.

The people were strange and she was timid. She was impressed and awed at the size of Kansas City; and Topeka was a larger city than she had ever seen. But that was not the destination—a little place called Burlingame, eighteen miles distant, was the chosen place; and the railroad ran through it. After they had found a little two-room house and established their home with the few things they had brought with them, and a little Number 7 cook stove and, as she said, "a few sticks of furniture" bought on time at the little secondhand furniture store, Father looked around for a means of providing the necessities of life.

The town consisted of a small frame hotel; a general store where you could buy yard goods like calico and unbleached muslin for sheets and pillow cases; a few drugs, such as castor oil, flaxseed for poultices, vaseline, and Dr. Miles Nerve Tonic; and, of course, groceries and meat part of the time. There was a hardware store that sold farm tools, nails, hammers, saws, and tinware, and a small prosperous pool hall where the men congregated and bought drinks and played cards.

The post office was a nook in the general store, so the effort of finding a job was difficult. Father still had the tired horse and the wagon. The wagon was a good one and at the time offered the only means of a livelihood, so he went to the livery barn and made arrangements to use it for headquarters. He bought a chair and small table and established an office near the front window. He painted a small crude sign on the front of the building. It read: "Coal, Wood, and Ice [I don't know where he got the ice], all kinds of hauling—Johnnie Hunt." And he was in business. One thing for sure, he wasn't lazy. He hauled coal from the mines and sold it in the town and some in the country, where most of his pay was in produce, feed for the horse, a chicken, a bag of potatoes or onions, and fresh vegetables in season, and in the fall apples and other fruit.

They had very little money to go on, but my father said he had never refused Mother a dollar when she asked for it, even if it was his last one. That first Christmas, Mother saw a display of mustache cups in the general store, and since my father always wore a small reddish mustache, she decided that was what she would give him for Christmas. She selected a rather large one. It had a small fancy bar near the edge on the inside to keep the mustache out of the coffee or tea. I remember the cup, which was one of the treasures that burned in the Victor fire years later. It was not pure white, but a sort of cream color, decorated with a conventional design. She had no money, so she charged it; the bill came to him later. He teased her about it. She said she had no money; how else could she give him a Christmas gift?

Then there was the high-pressure salesman who later sold her a little throw rug. It had pretty bright-red roses woven into it. They couldn't afford any such luxury, so Father was quite provoked about it. And when one of the children skidded on it and bumped his chin hard on the window sill, and since he had no love for that rug anyway, he picked it up and threw it out of the door. After he was gone Mother brought it in, rolled it up, and put it under the bed. Later she gave it away.

Father's one and only trade was butchering. His father had taught him the art of slaughtering, dressing, and cutting meat, so when he knew a farmer was planning to butcher, he would offer his services. And for pay, he came home with fresh meat and the promise of a piece of side meat and a few slices of ham when the meat was cured and smoked, and always some liver. At harvest time he would help any of the farmers, and often took Mother for the day. She wasn't so lonely after she had made a few friends in the country. When they drove into town for a day's shopping, they would come to her house for dinner and a visit.

On one of our visits to our friends, the Jacobses, we found they were adding an upper story to their house, and Mother climbed the rough, unfinished stairs to inspect the new room, telling me to stay downstairs. I disobeyed and followed her up, and when I reached the top two barking little black-and-tan dogs challenged me. I promptly tumbled all the way down, and in spite of my fright and bumps and bruises, Mother spanked me. I always said I fell down St. Jacob's stairs.

"Where there's a will there's a way," and while they didn't have much, they were getting along quite well; and the letters home were more cheerful.

Grandfather Hunt, however, was not well. He was still a young man in his early forties, but he found he was not able to lift and do the hard work he was accustomed to do. He and Grandmother had managed to live and save a little, but the Wisconsin venture had not proved to be the golden opportunity they had hoped for; and they missed their older son very much. So they asked about the possibility of their coming to Kansas and going into some small business. The hotel in Burlingame was not for sale, but there was a larger one in Carbondale, a small town about five miles from Burlingame, that was located very near the depot and was the stopping place for traveling men and train men. It also had a few regular guests. It was called the Shepherd House.

Late the next summer, the deal for the hotel was completed. They sold the property and their furnishings in Briddish Hollow, and Grandfather and Grandmother, Aunt Tillie, Aunt Amelia, Uncle Billie, and Aunt Della loaded the large wagon with their personal belongings and a few treasures and left for Kansas. Mother had written her folks about the baby expected in the fall; and when her mother heard his folks were leaving, she arranged to go with them for a visit, and to be with Mother when the baby arrived. She didn't know how she would get back home, but it didn't worry her much. Luckily a young man who had once lived near them, and had gone to Burlingame to establish a home, was returning to bring his schoolteacher bride back with him, and so Grandmother Doll went back home with him. Mother's people were not rovers; they were farmers, and Grandmother Doll was the only one who ever paid my parents a visit, and then only once. They stayed on their farms, cleared more acreage each year, and most of them prospered.

The hotel proved a success. Grandmother was a wonderful cook and manager, and the girls helped. Uncle Billie worked at a pool hall. He always said he wasn't well, and Grandmother babied him, so he got off easy where work was concerned.

Grandfather Hunt's health did not improve. They had heard of some natural hot springs in Pueblo, Colorado. While that seemed a great distance, Grandmother decided to take him there. (When Grandmother's mother died in England, she left her a small legacy.) But that didn't help, either, and the next year he died. He was about forty-seven. He had often told them that no male Hunt had ever reached the age of fifty, so from the very start of his illness he gave up. And that was no help, to say the least.

The doctor diagnosed his trouble as Bright's disease, and he claimed all his male ancestors had died of the same ailment. Uncle Billie died in his early forties, but my father must have inherited his mother's sturdy constitution, for he was eighty-two at the time of his death. One sister, Della, died at seventy-eight; Aunt Amelia, at seventy-five; and Aunt Tillie would in all probability have outlived all of them if the doctors had known our wonderful present-day drugs. She had a large carbuncle in the middle of her back that penetrated the spinal cord. She suffered for several weeks. Everything possible was done for her, but the infection spread through the blood stream and she died. Grandmother wore black for many years after Grandfather's death; and later in life, black and white, mostly small checked material.

She made her own dresses, and the pocket in the side seam must have been quite a large one, for she kept many things in it, among them always a supply of peppermint lozenges, and a little black purse with many nickels and pennies in it. To us children that pocket was a never-ending source of joy and anticipation, and its magic dried many a childish tear.

Grandmother Hunt wrote to her sister in England informing her of Grandfather's death, and she also told the other members of the family. One day a letter came from her father inviting Grandmother to return home and bring her children. All would be forgiven and she would share alike with the others. She did not answer the letter directly, but wrote her sister that since her husband had not been welcome during his lifetime, neither should his children be, from her point of view. When I visited

England with my English-born husband, David Heaton, I had no desire to go to Somersetshire and meet my Grandmother's people. I had inherited some of her pride, and my father was a Hunt and a tradesman.

Burlingame eventually had a doctor. His office was in his home, where he kept a small stock of drugs. His patients were scattered far and wide in the small near-by towns—Carbondale, Lawrence, Osage—and on the farms. He was a busy man; his name was Dr. Hallock. It was well he came at this time, because that winter an epidemic of diphtheria spread over the county and took its toll of little children in every home.

My home was no exception. There now were three little girls, Pearlie, Myrtie, Allie, and little John, age two. They were stricken the week preceding Christmas. Pearlie died first; and on Christmas day Allie and little John died. Since the disease was very contagious, all were buried the day they died. So the day after Christmas, just one lonely little girl was left of the four children. A friend who had no children had taken her to her home and started right away to spray her throat and do everything possible to prevent her catching the dread disease, but she did have a slight case.

Of course, Mother was heartbroken and lonely; and so was the little girl, Myrtie. Mother said she spent hours sitting at the gate post, too lonely to be shut in the now quiet house. Father missed those little children, too, especially the little boy, John, of whom he was very proud. He missed him sitting on the seat beside him on long rides. John had carried the whip and tapped the horse lightly with it, and talked all the time.

The little cemetery grew, that winter. Few families escaped the epidemic and the loss of children. Even isolated farms, where the family was voluntarily quarantined, suffered their share of loss. One farm family—Captain Lynch's—with whom our family visited, and who spent the day in our home on their trips to town, lost three of their four little ones. Mother said that on Christmas Eve Captain Lynch stayed and helped until the two little ones were laid away. She said the ground was so frozen at the cemetery that the one grave was dug deeper than usual, and both little coffins were placed in it.

My parents were so grateful for the help and sympathy of this wonderful friend and neighbor that when their next little girl was born, she was named for one of the little girls he had lost. That is why my name is Carrie Belle.

My father told me the treatment for diphtheria was to blow dry sulphur through a quill down the throat, and how he dreaded doing it, as the patient nearly choked to death every time.

Superstition and fear are dreadful things. One, a most heathenish superstition, had it that if a pregnant woman contracted what was known as three-day measles, or German measles, either the mother or the baby must die. That spring a new baby was expected; and very near the end of her time Mother contracted the dread disease. It was such a common belief that she was overcome with fear, and felt certain she would die. So when the healthy little boy was born, there was no question which one was to die; surely not my mother. So that ignorant doctor put the little fellow aside and gave Mother his undivided attention, and she really was desperately ill. My father said one of the hardest things he was ever called upon to do was to stand by and see that little baby die of neglect. He said he was such a lovely, healthy baby, and at first cried lustily. He said if he had insisted on the baby's being cared for, and Mother had died, not only would he have blamed himself, but all the superstitious people, including that ignorant doctor, would have blamed and condemned him. Of course, since Mother did live, he claimed that if he could do it over again that the baby would have lived. How could a man of intelligence like that doctor have believed such a silly and cruel superstition? And so they lost the little boy, who would have helped fill in the gap.

It was two years later, when Myrtie was seven, that I arrived —another girl. It was August 5, 1881, a terrifically hot night; and the few Negroes who had settled in Burlingame celebrated

President Lincoln's signing of the Proclamation of Emancipation
by dancing all night in the hall across the street. The noise
added to Mother's discomfort and upset her almost unbearably,
but there was nothing to be done about it.

Two years from the next October, a very welcome little baby
boy arrived. He was a fine bouncing boy and weighed twelve
pounds. Father wanted to name him William (Billie) for his
brother, but Mother had heard of a man who had recently
arrived in town by the name of Ogilvie, and that was the name
she chose. She called him Gilvie—others called him Gil—and
he always hated that name. When he grew up and went to
a new town alone, he changed it to George. I could not blame
him; no one but Mother liked his name. When he was two, a
little sister arrived, Neva. She was small and frail and sick most
of the year of her life. The doctor said she had lung fever.

We had moved to a larger house, and I remember a ravine
at the back. One morning I found a pretty blue morning-glory
and brought it to Neva. She smiled, and held it in her little
hand. When she was very ill, at the last, someone sat at the
side of her crib constantly; and Father asked me to sit there
once at mealtime. I didn't want to, but he said I wouldn't be
asked to sit again, that I wouldn't have a little sister for long.
I hadn't realized she was so ill, and sat quietly and watched
over her. She was very pale and seemed to be asleep. When
she died, a neighbor must have taken care of my brother Gil
and me; otherwise I am sure I would remember going to the
funeral.

Saturday afternoons we often drove to Carbondale and
stayed overnight at Grandmother's hotel. We loved it; we had
fun and we loved Grandmother. She was always kind to us,
and allowed us to play hide-and-seek all over the place with our
two cousins, Sam and Tillie, who lived at the hotel. There were
lots of hiding places. We would run in the long halls upstairs
and hide in one of the many rooms. When Mother objected to
our making so much noise, Grandmother said, "Let the children
play while they can. Soon they will take over more serious
things."

If you have never seen Kansas mud, you have never seen mud. There were no gravel roads, and the mud was the sticky kind. When you got stuck in it, you were really stuck. One Saturday when we were ready to go to Carbondale, Father said, "Now, the roads are very muddy, and we don't want to get stuck. So if we come to a very bad place, just keep quiet and leave it to me."

We came to a stretch of very muddy road, and when we were in the worst part of it, Mother said, "Oooo!"

The horses thought she said "whoa," and there we were—really stuck. We had to have help to get out, and Father's boots and Sunday clothes were covered with mud. He was provoked; but I remember we all laughed, and he did too.

Another playmate at Grandmother's was the beautiful big black dog, Dutch. He had a lovely coat, jet black with little curls all over. He was very friendly, and we were allowed to bring him inside to romp with us. One Saturday they told us he couldn't play, and not to go near him. They had him chained to his doghouse and a temporary fence put up some distance around him. He didn't seem sick and was happy to see us. They said a stray dog had run through the town and bitten a child and several dogs, including Dutch. It seemed bad enough for him to have been bitten without tying him up. We didn't understand; but the next time we went up there he was gone. He had rabies and they had had to shoot him.

Aunt Melia waited on the tables, and she treated us like any of the grown guests. She would rave over the different meats and desserts on the menu, and let us choose. Then she would say: "To drink: tea, coffee or milk."

We took coffee, something we never had at home. We put lots of sugar and cream in it, too. When we had a hot drink at home, it was cambric tea—hot water, sugar, and cream. She didn't tell on us, either.

One night while I was there, the big tomcat went into hiding so that he wouldn't be put out at bedtime. It was very cold outdoors, so the oven door in the large cook stove was left open to let the extra heat out into the kitchen as the house cooled off. Evidently Tom decided the oven would be a fine place to spend the night. And possibly he was right, but he hadn't reckoned with Aunt Amelia.

Early the next morning she came bustling into the kitchen to get breakfast. First, she closed the oven door; then she built a good fire in the stove and started mixing up a pan of biscuits. She kept hearing a cat cry so she opened the back door. The cat wasn't there, so back she went to her biscuits. But she was sure she could hear a cat crying. So she tried the cellar door. I guess that cat was almost roasted by the time she had the biscuits ready to bake, and opened the oven door. Old Tom leaped out of the oven and raced around and around the kitchen until Aunt Amelia was able to put down her biscuits and open the back door. Then out he went and raced across the prairie, and none of us ever heard of him again.

I do not remember when Uncle Grant, Aunt Tillie's husband, was sick; but I do remember going up to the hotel to his funeral. It was a very large funeral, and made quite an impression on me. I knew he must have been an important person, and an important person must be a soldier—an officer like our good friend Captain Lynch. So when I was in grade school studying history, I was sure he was General Grant, and told my teacher that General Grant was my uncle. I am sure she doubted it. Not too long ago I asked his daughter Tillie what was her father's rank in the army. She said she had never heard of his even being in the army. Oh, me!

About this time my father left on horseback for Texas. He had heard that the Texas longhorn cattle were good meat animals, and that they were a tough, sturdy breed, capable of living on prairie grass through the winter with little or no other feed. And since there was plenty of grazing land and very little grain or hay, several farmers thought it would be a good experiment to try to raise them.

He purchased several head and drove them part way, and then shipped them when he reached the first railroad. He told us that one of the animals had charged him when he was out with the rancher looking them over, and that he had been told to drop to the ground, as their horns were so long and straight that they couldn't reach him with them in that position. However, he was badly trampled before the rancher succeeded in rescuing him. I do not think the farmers had much luck with longhorns. When I visited my cousin's farm, not too long ago, there was no evidence of longhorns among his herds of milk cows, and he said he had never seen or heard of any.

That winter, my little brother Gil, who was three years old, had the measles, followed by pneumonia. His life was despaired of for days. Dr. Hallock spent most of his time working with my parents to save him. He put him in a sort of jacket made of flaxseed, a poultice both front and back. They were kept hot in the oven and changed often. The efforts saved his life, but he did not fully recover. During the next few months, he was thin and delicate. The doctor said neither the water nor the climate agreed with him, so my parents talked of leaving.

Kansas had not been very kind to them. All they had to show for fifteen years of hard work were two little girls, a sick little boy, and enough money to buy and equip the camp wagon. They called it a prairie schooner. They had five horses and the light buggy, and Mother said she had a few happy memories of the first four children. But mostly she had memories of days of sorrow and terror. She remembered when she baked bread on broiling hot days in a tiny kitchen with the doors and windows closed tight and the blinds drawn for fear of the begging bands of Indians; and when she couldn't endure the heat any longer she would pull up a blind only to look into the dirty, threatening faces of Indians. They would command her to open the window, by signs she had learned to understand. Then she would gouge out the insides of loaves of bread and fill the apertures with sorghum. She had heard that if anyone refused, the Indians would threaten to put little children on a hot stove until she complied with their demands.

Father said they would not do such things, but they always got the bread and sorghum, and the family ate the inside of the loaves she had gouged out while they were hot. It was mashed and doughy. Father told her she should simply pull the blind down again, and they would go away. He said they knew she was afraid of them.

Then there was the memory of the five little graves with the little marble headstones in the form of little lambs, with the names of the little children carved on them. Mother had a small white satin box tied with a blue ribbon; we called it the memory box. Sometimes she would show us what was in the box—five small plates taken from the little caskets with the names of the little children engraved on them, each plate wrapped in tissue paper, a couple of hair ribbons, a tiny toy or two, and the two pairs of earrings the little girls had worn when Aunt Melia pierced their ears without Mother's consent, and about which she was so angry.

Mother also had another box, one we were not so anxious to see. It was a brown tin box, the lid fastened tightly so that nothing spilled out, and it contained what she considered cures for all ills. Mother suffered from migraine headaches, so for her there was camphor and Carter's Little Liver Pills; vaseline for cuts and sores; castor oil, quinine; a few little rolls of clean cotton cloth for bandages; but last and most important of all was powdered rhubarb. That was her favorite remedy and our favorite hate.

Whenever little brother Gilvie was hard to get along with, and cried at every little provocation—look out! Out came that box with the rhubarb. The problem was to get him to take it. Whether I needed it or not, I had to have the first dose. If there had been any place to hide, I surely would have found it. At first, she mixed it in a large tablespoon with a little baking soda and water. Of course we cried, but she was persistent, and said, "Open wide and swallow it quick, and it won't taste so bad." And eventually my mouth would be full of the bitter dose and the taste of it. No amount of water seemed to wash the taste away. Next would come the battle with Gilvie and the final result.

Mother finally devised a way to get it down without leaving such a bad taste. She took a little square of tissue paper, put the powder and soda in it, and twisted the corners tightly.

Result, not once did that paper capsule go down whole; it broke in our mouths, and we had a mouthful of the bitterest powder possible. It took hours to wash it down, and it left the bitter taste just the same. The powder was a golden brown, and to this day no paint, no matter how shiny, and no fabric that shade, has ever been attractive to me. Instantly I think, "Rhubarb!"

Father said he had a scar to carry away. Once when he was putting up a stove, a length of stovepipe fell and cut a deep gash across his nose. It had soot in it, and some particles got in the cut and wouldn't wash out; so he had a dark line on his nose permanently.

True, they had made some good friends who did not like the idea of their leaving. And then there was the family at Carbondale. But Aunt Tillie had remarried, and with her husband and two children had moved out on a farm. Aunt Della had married a young merchant from Wisconsin who had come to Carbondale on business, and met her, and they had gone back to North Andover to live, where he had a general store. So Grandmother, Aunt Melia, and Uncle Billie decided they would follow us when we were settled in the new location. Vilas, Colorado, was considered as the possible destination. Mother favored Pueblo on account of the mineral water and the hope it would prove beneficial for the little boy's health. And so once more my parents set out on the long trail awinding, with hope in their hearts to find the pot of gold at the rainbow's end, the land of their dreams, and the never-to-be-forgotten long trip in the camp wagon.

CHAPTER IV

THE DECK

Science tells us that "thoughts are things," and since thoughts are expressed in words, then words have a very definite meaning, and automatically become "things."

There is one word that has had an outstanding place in my life, and around which all of my early life revolves; in fact, it has been closely associated with my entire life and memories. That word is "deck," my father's "deck." To him and to us, his family, the word has a significance all its own. It was not a ship's deck, but one built to economize room, and it had various uses.

Father's first deck is the most vivid in my memory. (He built many more later.) He built it with great care, and only after much planning, in a camp wagon, or prairie schooner. It consisted of two wide shelves securely hinged to the interior sides of the wagon, about two-thirds distance from the floor, so that they could be let down during the day and raised at night. Two or three strong slats were fitted under them in some way to hold the shelves firmly in place when they were raised for use. Then a mattress and bedding, which during the day were piled on top of the mattress in the bottom of the wagon, were placed on the deck and a second comfortable bed was complete.

I was about five years old when my father built our first deck, but I remember it as if it were yesterday. With my older sister, who was twelve, I occupied the deck at night in the middle of the wild vast prairie, but the sense of security we felt up there, knowing that our father, mother, and little brother were sleeping directly under us, was warmer and more complete than any other I can remember. It never occurred to us that our bed had no springs, and we would fall asleep as soon as we crept in. There was no way for us to see the stars or the moon, but, oh, that heavenly lullaby on the canvas top when it rained! Yes, we were both comfortable and happy on our first deck. Indeed, we were comfortable and happy under the deck, too; for the double mattress on the floor of the wagon made a wonderful place to rest during the day, on the long, hard ride we were about to take.

I was too young to remember all that led up to our moving from the small town in Kansas, where I was born, but the chief reason was my little brother's health. It was April when we started. Sometime during the preceding winter he had contracted measles and then pneumonia, from which he seemed unable to recover completely. The country doctor advised a change of climate and of water. It seemed that the water was especially bad in that locality, and the doctor said that good water was quite necessary for his recovery.

Kansas at that time, seventy-five years ago, was really frontier country and my parents considered themselves pioneers. But Colorado, our much-discussed destination, was really the "jumping-off place." Since water seemed to be our most important requirement, however, Pueblo became our final objective. Why Pueblo I'll never know. Perhaps the good doctor had heard of the natural hot springs in that vicinity and had confused them with artesian wells. Maybe there were artesian wells there at that time. I don't know. It just seems odd to me now that we should have undertaken a journey of such proportions in order to drink Pueblo water.

I have many fine friends in Pueblo and hasten to add that I have nothing against Pueblo water. I've just never noticed anything particularly salubrious about it.

My father at that time was in the livery-stable business, which I suppose had something to do with the number of horses and the extra buggy we brought along. The horses hitched to the wagon were larger than the other three, but were really too small for the heavy load. I distinctly remember the gray mare as one of them; she was a great favorite and very gentle. The two matched sorrels hitched to the new light buggy were my father's pride and joy. My sister drove them all the way. I rode with her, and we led the young buckskin saddle horse behind us. The excuse for having him along was that in an emergency, such as illness or an Indian attack, my sister, who was an excellent rider, could go fast for help. My father evidently felt that she should have a swift mount; for, as I recall, the distances between villages, and indeed between houses, were very great.

For some reason Father had built the camp wagon in Carbondale, which was only a short distance from Burlingame; and I remember the light buggy being loaded, including the memory box, and, sorry to say, the detestable medicine box.

My father and sister left a day or two ahead of the rest of the family. Mother and we children went by train—a wonderful train! The ride was short; and as near as I can figure out there was no baggage car. So much to my mother's embarrassment, a coop of three large white hens and a rooster that had been given to me by my old friend the sea captain, who once had had a small daughter after whom I was named, had to ride in the coach with us. Whether the chickens escaped accidentally or whether I deliberately let them out, I am not sure. But I vividly recall the excitement when all four chickens flew the coop and squawked the length of the car before we were able to corral them. The escapade nearly cost me my chickens. When we joined my father and sister at the end of our train ride, it took a lot of coaxing and tears before Father finally fastened the coop beside the tiny sheet-iron camp stove on the back of the wagon. Among other things I have forgotten is the ultimate fate of those chickens. But it seems to me that on the way across the prairie, they disappeared one by one.

The excitement of the start and the first few days on the road are blurred in my memory. There seemed to be just one big surprise after another, all mixed up in our great adventure. The first stop that is clear to me was at Vilas, Colorado; and there was some talk of our staying there. Looking back, I don't know how my father could have supported a family there. All I recall of the village were a tall frame house and a saloon.

By the way, do they still decorate cigar-box lids with those beautiful pictures of gorgeous ladies? My sister and I were entranced with those we found at the rear door of the Vilas saloon. We slipped one of each into every available corner of the buggy and wagon, only to have them used to start the camp-stove fire the following morning. But if Mother was ruthless, we were persevering; and after breakfast the hunt for pictures would be on again at the rear door of the saloon.

The tall frame house must have been a hotel. I remember the ladder that led to a large unfinished loft full of beds. It was here that Mother decided Vilas was not a suitable place for us to stay. The woman who ran the place called us "kids." Mother had never heard that word applied to anything except young goats. So we moved on.

At first, it must have been my sister and I in the light buggy who were in the lead, where it should have been easy for my parents to watch us. But after a while we began to go so much faster than the heavy wagon that we were often out of sight over the rises in the trail. Finally, after repeated warnings of danger, and of the anxiety we were causing, my father made us ride behind the wagon. This arrangement turned out to be much better for us later, but we were in disgrace for a time.

I suppose that most children have the desire to capture wild birds, especially young ones in a nest. My sister and I were not exceptions, and there was a great variety of birds along the way. We often talked about getting a nest of birds, but Father said the birds would die, as we would not know how or where to get the right kind of food for them. This sort of talk, of course, did not impress us at all. Kansas, as usual, abounded in grasshoppers. So during a short stop, one fine day, when my sister discovered a nest within reach in a low-hanging tree, she just couldn't resist taking it down, and we smuggled it between us on the buggy seat. That day, instead of being able to push the wagon a little faster toward Colorado, my poor father and mother had to keep stopping to look back for us. Sometimes we would be out of their sight behind a small hill, but at other times they could see me out of the buggy, running wildly across the prairie and making passes at the ground with my sunbonnet. Mother also objected to the bonnet being used for such purposes, as she had spent precious time making it. (She had also made one for herself and Myrtie, and even one for little Gil, who objected strenuously to such feminine apparel. But in spite of the bonnet he still developed large brown freckles across his nose.) That night, of course, they found out that I had been hunting grasshoppers and warned us sternly against such private expeditions while traveling.

But those young birds, about feathered out, had terrific appetites. Even after we had crammed a big grasshopper down each big open mouth, there was an almost immediate demand for more. So naturally we would have to disregard our parents' warning and loiter behind so that I could capture some more food.

After a few days, during which our progress had slowed down considerably, my parents, one morning, hurried us from one small task to another, and then pulled out in the big wagon before we were ready to leave. Fearful of being left behind, we forgot our birds and did not even think of them until we were several miles on our way. I still remember how we reproached each other, and wept. Later, we found out that we had been hurried intentionally, and Father tried to make it a little easier for us to bear our loss by telling us that other birds would take care of ours, even better than we were able to. I wonder.

We always stopped an hour at noon for lunch—cold biscuit and maybe jelly or cold bacon. We would be tired of riding, and the horses needed food and rest. Father would unhitch them and remove their harness, and since they were tired and we could watch them, he did not hobble them. The first thing they did was to lie down and roll over. We played a game with them to see which one rolled over the most times. Father said for each complete roll over they were worth a hundred dollars.

We carried enough water for each horse to have a small drink, if there was no other source; then a canvas bag, known as a nose bag, with oats in it, was fastened over each head, and they would find every grain. It took them the full hour to finish their lunch. When all were fed and rested, we would be on our way again.

We always tried to stop early, as there were many chores connected with setting up our overnight camp. The horses had to be unhitched and hobbled out on the prairie, where they could graze overnight on the buffalo grass, which was short and sweet and very nutritious. Of course, Father also carried a supply of oats, which he thought they required to maintain their strength to pull the heavy wagon. Then the camp stove had to be unloaded and set up with a couple of lengths of stove pipe, while we children gathered buffalo chips for the fire. Mother insisted that she have the light of the sun to prepare dinner, as evening was the only time we had a hot dinner cooked on the little sheet-iron stove; and I have never since tasted such wonderful biscuits as the ones that came out of that tiny oven.

Occasionally we had to travel late to find a suitable place, and then Mother would have to prepare dinner by the aid of a lantern, and we would have to eat by its light. Besides the fact that it gave a poor light, we were always afraid that it might attract the attention of Indians or marauders, for although we never saw an Indian on the long trip, we did see torn-up spots on the prairie where wagon trains had been attacked and destroyed, and we heard terrifying tales of recent massacres. Mother was deathly afraid of Indians, and her fear was naturally transmitted to us children. I am not sure whether I actually remembered visits we had from wandering Indians in the then little frontier town of Burlingame, or had heard the older people discussing them; but I do remember Mother's keeping the doors and windows shut and the blinds drawn on hot sultry days, and nearly smothering all of us.

On one of our late-stop nights, Mother was quite upset over getting dinner in semidarkness, and worry about having the lantern lit so long caused her to sleep restlessly. Suddenly she started to scream. My sister and I were terrified. I can remember Father's exact words: "God Almighty! What's the matter now?"

Father was more afraid of keeping a loaded gun around than

of any danger that might threaten, so instead of a gun he always kept a large, sharp butcher knife handy. While she was shouting, he reached for his knife and prepared for the struggle. Then Mother had to explain sheepishly that she had seen a man's arm inside the canvas at the back of the wagon, only to find that when Father moved he took the arm with him. That was the closest we came to an Indian attack.

We never had any trouble with wild animals. Father and Mother told us later that they had seen a number of buffalo, but always in the distance. In the evening we often saw what we thought were wild dogs, but when we asked about them at a settlement we were told that they were coyotes.

Since we had no gun we were not prepared to shoot a sage hen or pheasant, and we rarely saw one. We did miss fresh fruit and vegetables, especially Mother, who was very fond of cabbage and greens. So one evening when we were camped and supper was over, she went for a short walk and discovered what she thought was a turnip patch. There was no fence, so while she did not feel she was trespassing, she was guilty of taking something that did not belong to her. She came back to camp with her apron full of turnips, with the tops left on for greens. She felt guilty about it, especially when Father teased her.

The next morning we had traveled only a short distance when we came to a small house, and as was our custom we stopped to inquire if we could buy milk, butter, eggs, or anything they might have to sell us. Mother asked them about the turnip patch. They said yes, it belonged to them, but they were not turnips but rutabagas, and we were welcome to all we wanted. Then she confessed and offered to pay, but they refused, and said we could go back and get some more. I think she would have liked some more, but we were not in the habit of retracing our steps, as the wagon was really too heavy for the light team to haul. That night was our first experience with rutabagas. We liked them fairly well, but not the greens. They were bitter, but Mother thoroughly enjoyed both.

Water, of course, was our big problem, but fortunately for us it was spring when we went through. And we nearly always found a camping place not too far from a stream, or at least a trickle. We carried some water, but never enough for even one day. We were told that when the run was made to Oklahoma, at the time the "strip" was opened to homesteaders, shortly before we came through, there were long stretches where there were no streams or springs at all, and the almost destitute farmers along the way sold water from their wells to the thirsty travelers at twenty-five cents for each adult and animal. Purchasers, however, were allowed to fill any containers they might have with them. Some queer combinations were seen at the farmers' wells. Some pushed wheelbarrows or pulled small, toylike wagons; others led one or more starving horses; some had a patient ox or two, or perhaps a weary mule. And one traveler who appreciated the value of milk had a cow teamed up with his old horse.

One other thing I remember about our prairie trip; and because of it, until I was many years older, I could inform all the other curious children where our parents found our little brothers and sisters. One day we saw a little hammock hanging from a tree, and in it was a tiny baby, sound asleep. My sister and I wanted to take it along with us, but Mother said we had no place for it to sleep, and Father reminded us of how little money we had. But they promised that we would get one later, when we had a house in which to live. When I was older, Mother told me that she had seen the baby's mother washing clothes in a creek near by, and that there was a wagon, or a shack, hidden in the trees.

The next small town we came to in Colorado was Lamar. Compared to Vilas it seemed like a city. I remember a post office in the front of a cigar store, where we again gathered our beautiful boxes with the pictures of grand ladies on the lids, a hotel of sorts, a general store, the inevitable livery stable, and a few shacks. There were no trees; only the same barren countryside all around. Evidently Lamar did not appeal to Father and Mother, so after a few days we continued slowly toward Pueblo.

By this time the horses were very tired and footsore, and Father fully intended to settle in Pueblo. I don't remember much about the town, but after we had been there only a few days, our little brother became much worse, and Father was convinced that it was not the place for us. So when someone told us about the new town of Colorado Springs, and its wonderful water, we were once more on our way.

My sister and I were delighted to continue the journey, as we were enjoying the trip. For us each new day was an adventure, although the country out of Pueblo was much the same as that through which we had just passed and to which we were accustomed in Kansas—just miles and miles of sagebrush and cactus, and a little dirt road always leading West. But as we drew nearer to Colorado Springs, we began to see the mountains more clearly. Then we caught our first glimpse of Pikes Peak. Mother was enraptured, and there was no doubt in her mind that she had reached the end of the trail.

"I want to live and die right here," she said, "at the foot of that beautiful mountain!"

She and my father are buried in the little West Side cemetery at the foot of the mountains in the shadow of Pikes Peak.

CHAPTER V

COLORADO CITY
(Old Town)

If Vilas was a wide place in the road, Lamar a little town, and Pueblo a big town, Colorado Springs was a city. Were we ever thrilled! And wonder of wonders, men were laying the tracks of the horse-drawn streetcars on Colorado Avenue just west of the Rio Grande tracks, where we were held up by closed gates while a train passed. We passed through and continued as far as the point where the tracks were being laid, and a little farther. It had started to rain, but we didn't mind. We were driving into Colorado City. We had arrived. It was late in the afternoon of May 24, 1887.

If Colorado Springs was a city, Colorado City was a metropolis. There were only four houses on Colorado Avenue between the two towns, but the business district was impressive, with buildings on both sides of the street for at least a full block.

Soon the buildings tapered off to only two or three in a block, and then there was the unbroken meadow. But on the hillside we discovered a tiny abandoned shack. It had only half a roof, but Father and Mother decided that it offered enough shelter for us to set up the little camp stove and prepare dinner. While they were still deciding where to put things in the little shack, a gentleman knocked on what should have been the door. He said that he and his wife lived alone in a five-room house at the foot of the hill. He was so insistent that we stay with them for at least the night that Father reloaded the camp stove and a few other things, and we drove back down the hill with the gentleman.

To us the house was a mansion, and those two kindly people just one step below the angels. The man was short and squarely built, with a short, stubby beard and eyes that twinkled merrily. His wife was short and plump and soft and kind. Their name was Baker, and I know they were the most hospitable people I have ever met.

Mother, Father, and my little brother were to occupy the spare bedroom. So while Mother prepared dinner, Father brought in a mattress from the wagon and made a bed for my sister and me on the front-room floor. And all the time Mr. and Mrs. Baker were talking to all of us. The way they visited, you would have thought they had always known us.

The next day, Mr. Baker and Father took the buggy and went out to look over the situation, while Mrs. Baker and Mother held a talkfest. Mother was so excited and happy that she did most of the talking. The men were gone all day, and when they returned they, too, were talkative, having discovered that beer was plentiful and cheap. Mother was quite provoked and was reminding Father of our dwindling reserves when Mrs. Baker had some sort of "spell," to which she was subject whenever she became upset. The only way she could be brought out of the "spell" was by having her husband pound her on the back in a certain way. We children were terrified, for we were not used to seeing a woman treated so roughly. But she recovered quickly and assured us that this treatment was the only thing that could pull her out of such attacks, and that it didn't hurt her at all. At first we were rather skeptical, but as the days went by we learned that Mr. Baker would never deliberately do anything to hurt his wife. They were very devoted to each other.

After the uproar caused by Mrs. Baker's "spell" and its cure had subsided, the men told us the news they had garnered in their tour of Colorado City's numerous saloons. Everyone was talking, they said, about the big gold strike at the Madonna Mine in Monarch, Colorado, about one hundred and twenty-five miles farther west. So far as Father and Mr. Baker were concerned, we were already on our way. And sure enough, within a few days all of us, including the Bakers, were setting off into the mountains to make our fortunes.

Myrtle and I still occupied the deck, but to this day I can't figure out where the rest of them slept. Perhaps, since the rain was over, they took along another mattress and the men slept under the wagon. Anyway, I know everyone managed to sleep. And how we all did eat!

The scenery was incredibly beautiful through the pine-covered mountains, and our new friends were so congenial that we all seemed to be one happy family on a long outing in God's most wonderful picnic grounds. Almost immediately my little brother began to improve. The invigorating mountain air brought color to his wan little cheeks, and he drank quantities of the delicious soft water we found in the mountain springs and streams, fed by the melting snow.

Our route was up the famous Ute Trail. And at that time it was a trail, the one the Indians followed from their distant camps to find buyers for their hides in Denver, where they bought their few supplies, which they carried back again over the same trail into the mountains. Over this trail they brought their sick to the springs in the tiny town of Manitou, named, according to the legend we heard, for one of their chiefs who had been brought there many years before to bathe in and drink the mineral water that flowed from any place they cared to dig a hole. The aging chief not only recovered his health, but claimed to be completely rejuvenated, with all his youthful vigor restored. Many others who were not really sick, so the story went, also came and were made young again.

The trail was not quite where the beautiful highway of today is enjoyed by summer tourists, but it was in the same canyon, only higher on the side of the mountain, so that the rains and swollen streams would not wash it away. And it was very narrow. It had been built and kept up by the Indians, who were not fond of work and who really didn't need a very wide trail. They generally traveled single file; first the men on horseback, then the horses packed with provisions and pelts for trade, and finally the women, trudging along on foot, usually with loads on their backs, unless one or the other happened to be carrying a papoose.

On the rare occasions when we met another wagon, the men

would get out and consult with each other about which wagon would have to be backed to a place wide enough for the two to pass. The shelf trail was very high, and it looked a long way down to the swift stream below. Mother would become so nervous on these occasions that she would cry; and taking my little brother in her arms, she would walk on ahead while the men maneuvered the wagons. It seemed that we were always the ones who had to back around the curves with our heavy wagon and the buggy, as the horses the others were driving were always broncs not broken to back up. Their owners probably thought they had done well to break them to go forward.

Getting by other travelers didn't worry me too much, as it gave Mr. Baker more time to whittle out the most marvelous little knives, forks, and spoons from small pieces of wood that he had brought along for that purpose. And he had bribed me into lightening the load for the tired horses by promising that, if I walked with him, he would carve me a full set. He had ample time to make good his promise, as I think I walked all the way to Monarch.

Eventually we reached the top of Wilkerson Pass and looked down on the vast level valley of South Park, surrounded on all sides by mountains. The snow-capped peaks ahead were very high, and appeared to rise straight up from the flat green valley. Our road stretched out across it like a narrow ribbon, without a house or any other building on either side. And our progress across the valley seemed both unending and uninteresting. Except for the lure of the mountains ahead, it was much like the flat, unvarying country we had gone through in Kansas and eastern Colorado. Our trip over the Ute Pass had spoiled us, that is, all except Mother. The only redeeming feature about it that I could see was that the horses had almost no uphill pulls until we approached the mountains. And when we had almost reached them, we found that they did not rise up stark and straight from the valley floor, but were approached by foothills and separated from them by Trout Creek Pass.

Incidentally, why the pass was ever called Trout Creek has always puzzled me. I have lived here many years now and driven over that pass hundreds of times, and usually everything in that pass is dust dry. At times, indeed, a tiny creek does appear, but it is never more than a trickle, and I doubt that even a fingerling trout could find enough water in which to swim.

The evening we arrived at the top of this pass was a memorable one. It gave us a spectacular view of still another range of snow-capped mountains, especially of the Collegiate Peaks of Harvard, Yale, and Princeton, and of a truly beautiful valley through which the Arkansas River wound its way. But I remember it for another reason.

After the long day on the road, we children were always glad to climb out of the wagon (if, indeed, I had been in it) and explore everything around our camp. My little brother loved to run around the wagon, sit on the ground, and dig in the soft sand. On this night he came to the wagon where Mother was cooking and asked her for a knife. She gave him a dull old case knife, and he ran off to play.

Suddenly we heard him scream. What he had thought was a nice big sand pile turned out to be an anthill, the home of those big, vicious red ants. They had evidently resented his sitting on their home and slashing it every which way with his knife. Poor little fellow! When Mother reached him, he was covered with ants that were stinging him unmercifully. A dishpan of water happened to be heating on the stove for the evening dishes. Mother stripped his clothes off as fast as she could, added soda to the warm water, and plumped him into it. How he did cry! And he was sick for several days. The soda-water bath did help, however, probably as much as anything Mother could have bought if we had been near a drugstore.

We had hoped to reach Monarch the next night, but we did not realize how bad the road was nor how steep it was in places. The horses had not rested sufficiently from their long trip to Colorado City, and their load was heavy. So it was several days before we drove into the tiny, wildly excited town of Monarch, where everyone talked only of claims and gold.

The settlement consisted mostly of cabins. The one street

ran from east to west with two or three larger buildings on its north side. One of them was a store with rooms upstairs that were rented to the crowds of men who had flocked in when the rich strike was reported. A small stream ran through the narrow valley on the south side of the street, where there were a number of small, one-story buildings with basements of a sort that faced the stream, and from which one could look up the almost sheer side of the mountain and see the fast-growing dump of the Madonna Mine surrounded by dozens of small holes in the mountain, where prospectors had started to work their claims, hoping to find an outcropping of the rich vein.

It was in one of the these single-room basements that we cooked and slept. The men slept in the wagon as the nights were very cold. The snow was not yet gone from the north side of the mountain, but we gathered bright wildflowers that grew at the very edge of the melting snow banks.

I very soon discovered a little girl about my age who lived in the next basement. One day she told me how they had stayed in their underground room for several days during an Indian attack. Of course, I relayed this information to the folks at home. Mother and Mrs. Baker had never been too enthusiastic about the town, with its miserable living conditions and the extreme wildness of the surrounding country, but this announcement, implying the presence of hostile Indians, brought to an end any chance of our locating there. Soon we were on our way back to Colorado City and the Bakers' comfortable home.

On our return we made a little detour. Instead of going directly to the bridge across the Arkansas River, about two miles east of Buena Vista, we drove about ten miles down the river to the larger town of Salida. As our finances were now very low, just forty cents, to be exact, Father reluctantly decided to sell the light buggy and team. We made camp near the town, and the men drove off to find a buyer.

Salida, like all the western towns we had seen, had a great many saloons. One of these offered a huge schooner of beer, invitingly topped with white foam, and a free lunch, for five cents. Soon Father had only thirty cents, and then less, and there could be no question now about selling the team. When the men returned to camp, Father had forty dollars. It seemed like a fortune.

Next day we started "home," as we called it. I didn't have to walk quite as much as I had coming, as it was now downhill more of the way; besides my wooden "silver set" was now complete, and no one came forward with any new bribes. However, there were now seven to ride in the camp wagon. The return trip was uneventful and not so slow, but poor Mother worried all the way about coming down over Ute Pass; and indeed I believe that the trip down was a little worse than up, as we were now on the outer edge of the shelf. We arrived at the bottom right side up, however, and soon we were happy to be at home in Colorado City.

And now we said good-by to our first deck. Father sold the camp wagon and one of the horses, but not the gray mare. Father noticed that she had developed a cough, and he now turned her out to pasture for the long rest she deserved. Every day he would take her a pail of oats, and find her waiting at the gate for him. But one day when he came with the oats, she was nowhere to be seen. He found her lying just over a little hill, our faithful, good old horse. Father said she had died of lung fever. We all missed her. And soon afterward the saddle horse broke his hind leg. He caught it some way in the fence. Father had him hung in a sort of hammock and his leg in splints. In spite of this care, he died in a short time, and now we had no horse.

Father rented a four-room house down on the avenue, just across the street from the little log house that they say had been Colorado's first Capitol, occupied at that time by two Chinese, who used it for a laundry. Our new home had a little picket fence around the front and one side. On the other side was a long building, which like all the other buildings on both sides of the street, except three, was a saloon and gambling house. As far as we children were concerned, however, it could have been a church. We were not allowed outside our gate except

with one or both of our parents, and we were so interested in
what went on right in our own yard that we scarcely noticed
the busy street in front.

Father had bought us a nanny goat and little wagon, and
since Gilvie was now recovering rapidly, and the doctor advised
that he be kept outdoors most of the day, we spent most of our
time with the goat. She was very gentle and must have had a
kid recently. We harnessed, unharnessed, and milked her all day
long. Without bothering about straining or pasteurizing, we
drank the milk just as it was out of an old tin dipper that hung
on the outdoor hydrant. And the roses bloomed in little Gilvie's
cheeks, and he burned as brown as an Indian. Mother tied an
old sunbonnet on my head to preserve my ladylike complexion,
but by the end of summer I was practically black.

How Father maneuvered enough money to rent and meagerly
furnish the house, buy us the goat, and start a café in a little
narrow store building in the block, I do not know. He always
said he could start a business on a shoestring, and that must
have been about all he had. He was never lazy, and with the
help of one chef he really made money. Gamblers and fortune
hunters who flock into a new wide-open town have money and
spend it freely. Prices were not like what they are now; but
since it was the one and only place to eat, there was no question
about the cost of a meal, and everything in the way of delicacies
available was prepared and sold.

An outstanding customer was gambler Jack Diamond. He
was a flashily dressed person—wore a fancy vest always, and
carried a gold-headed cane. When he was flush and his luck
good, he paid fancy prices for fancy meals; but when he had
a run of bad luck Father trusted him. One day he got into an
argument with Father's brother, Uncle Billy, and when Father
objected he struck him over the head with the cane. It cut a
deep gash several inches in length and required several stitches.
He either paid for his meals after that or went without.

One morning a man came to the house with a crate of
pigeons that we children hoped would be pets for us. But
Father ruthlessly slaughtered them, and the chef boiled them in

Mother's wash boiler, fried them, took them to the café, and put each one on a piece of toast. That day "quail on toast" was on the menu—at a dollar an order. In those days that was a fabulous price, but the supply was far short of the demand.

At one time Father had been a butcher, so it wasn't long before he branched out with a meat market in a small building he put up in our front yard between our house and the saloon, facing the avenue. He had built a shack down by the creek where he bought and butchered the meat for the shop and the café.

When we began to tire of Nanny, she suddenly disappeared, but one day we found her hide at the slaughterhouse. The "lamb chops" must have been on the tough side; but like the "quail," I am sure they found a ready sale. We probably had some at our own table.

The meat market was a small, one-room building, but it was not too small to curtain off a front corner to exhibit a petrified man, at ten cents a look. Father either shared in the receipts or charged the exhibitor a rental fee. At any rate, as members of the family, we children were privileged to go in and look at him free as often as we liked. He lay in a coffin and was supposed to have been an adult; but as I remember, he must either have been a very small man or have shrunk in the process of petrification. He was quite gray in color, but was realistic enough. A sign on the coffin said not to touch him. But since I had many opportunities to slip in alone, my curiosity finally got the better of me and I touched his face. It was stone cold and the experience made me a little sick. And it was several days before I could wash away the smell of putty from my hands. To this day the smell of putty brings back to mind a picture of that petrified man.

Another thing I recall about the meat market is the time Father left me in charge of it. He evidently was going to be gone only a few minutes, but he was expecting one of the Chinese who ran the laundry across the street to come over for his usual order of pork chops. He had already wrapped them, and when he called me into the shop he showed me the little

package on the table, and told me to give it to "John Chinaman" if he should come for it before he returned. I was scared
stiff. Father discounted my fear, if he noticed it at all, as the
normal reaction of a little girl at being left alone in a responsible
position. What he didn't know was that we children had been
entertaining ourselves by calling the Chinamen names. I still
remember a little rhyme we would chant before their laundry:

> Ching chong Chinaman stole my wood;
> Ching chong Chinaman ain't no good!

Then, when the Chinamen would appear at the door, we would
run as fast as we could. It was an exhilarating pastime, but I
had not anticipated a situation like this, where I would have to
face one of them alone in a little room.

Father had just left when the door of the laundry opened
and John Chinaman came out. From the screen door I watched
him cross the street. Suddenly I had an inspiration. I locked
the door with the hook-and-eye latch, and then just stood there.
John came directly to the door and tried to open it. Then he
asked me to unlock it. Then he shook the door. When he
stopped shaking it, he demanded that I unlock it. He must have
repeated the performance several times, but the door and I both
stood firm. I was convinced, with some reason, that John would
have loved to murder me on the spot if he could just get that
door open. So through the whole ordeal I gave a silent imitation of the petrified man in the corner. Free of charge, too.
At last Father returned. I unhooked the door and streaked for
home past the two of them. It was the fastest I have ever run
in my life. In fact, I probably set a record for the twenty-foot
dash.

We had lived in the cottage only a few months when the
owner decided to tear it down and build a saloon. There were
only seventeen in the block by then, and it was obvious to him
that the good citizens of Colorado City could well use another.
So we moved into a two-room house that Father built behind
the café. He built it in such a way that it could easily be

moved later, as by this time we were prospering to the extent that Father could begin planning a house big enough for the growing family. But it was in this tiny house that we were given the baby Mother had promised us on the camp-wagon trip— a dear little boy. Mother named him Burt. We considered him most attractive. And we weren't the only ones who thought so. When Mother carried him down the street, the pretty ladies who lived just behind us would follow her closely, and beg her to lift the soft veil it was then customary to keep over an infant's face when outdoors, to protect him from cold and colic, so that they could see his big brown eyes. My, how those girls admired him! They were young, and Mother said that they were lonely and homesick. I found this hard to believe, as they looked very much like the gorgeous ladies we found pictured on our prized cigar-box lids—all dressed up in frilly, long red dresses, with their hair cut short and curled all over their heads.

As a matter of fact, we were living in the very center of one of the toughest frontier towns in America. With all the saloons, gambling houses, gunmen, and adventurers, I suppose the sporting houses were inevitable. Colorado City had an extensive collection, and they were all directly behind us. Yet in all the time we lived there I must admit I cannot recall seeing a single incident or hearing a single word that would have offended the most exacting moralist.

Indeed, two other little girls and I once spent the afternoon at the big sporting house right across the alley from our back yard. The madam had a little girl our age, and she had invited us in. We had a wonderful time playing with her toys. And her mother seemed delighted to have us. I recall that she gave us ice cream, cake, and all the candy we could eat. Mother, of course, was horrified when she found out where I had been, and Father was very stern when he came home and heard about it. I couldn't understand why I wasn't allowed to play with Madam Laurabelle's little girl, or, for that matter, with the other two little girls unless we stayed either at their house or at mine.

Of course, Mother and Father were quite right; but even in later years when I could understand those things, I always felt that there was something good about Laurabelle. As time went on, many kind things that she had done for others became known; and many I suppose will be forever unknown. She was generous to a fault, and always gave liberally to every good cause. But it was her continuing, secret little acts of personal charity that gradually, despite her previous profession, gave her some standing in the community. Her last act upon earth was typical.

A blind man, Dusty McCarty, lived near her in later years, and Laurabelle was not content with simply giving him money on which to live; she was determined that he should have a chance to see again. So she and her niece took him to Denver in her car to see an eye specialist and arrange for an operation. On the return trip she and her niece were both killed in an automobile accident near Castle Rock.

And then there was the never-to-be-forgotten fire. One very cold, windy March night came what was termed "the crimson fire." This occurred at the close of Old Town's heyday and destroyed the famed red-light district. It started at R.M.'s (a Negro madam) or close by, and due to the terrific wind spread to the entire section between what is now Twenty-fifth and Twenty-sixth streets and Cucharras. I was not there at the time, so for a description of the fire and the events of that night, I am quoting an article written by my cousin Clarion Taylor, who was an eyewitness and participated in fighting the fire. It was entitled "It Happened on a Windy Night."

Toward the close of Old Town's hey-day, after Colorado City had seen its boom, came the Crimson Fire—the destruction of Old Town's famed Red Light District.

One who experienced the wind and cold of that March night, when citizens all over town were struggling in the bitter cold to protect their homes by spraying water on sides and roof, could never forget the tragic event.

Nor could Preacher B. of the First —— Church ever forget, and certainly Jack Diamond remembered it poignantly. But to get on with the story.

Grandma (Mary Ann) Doll

Grandpap Doll (Josef Dahl)

Grandma (Mary Ann) Hunt

Grandpa (John H.) Hunt

Father and Mother on their wedding day: John Henry, age twenty, and Amanda Ellen, age eighteen

Father *(left)* with his brother Billie and sisters Amelia, Matilda, and Della

Me, sister Myrtle Mary, and brother Ogilvie just before we set out in the camp wagon

Mother at the time we left
Kansas

Me, at four years of age

Aunt Tillie and her children, Tillie and Sam, and
Uncle Grant—who I thought was *General* Grant

The three undertakers: brother Burt, my father, and
brother Gil

Me on my eightieth birthday, August 5, 1961

Like most early-day western cities the time comes when the "boom" passes and later tenderfeet begin trodding those earlier paths so laboriously pioneered by the earlier arrivals. Such was the history of Colorado City—as the earlier "greats" passed on their way, reformers came to save the remaining citizens from crime and iniquity. As their number increased they gradually took over the reins of government, not primarily for saving their own souls but to make it rough on the souls of those with whom they disagreed. In their concept of "reformation" they proceeded on the theory that an outward show of religion was the essential thing, overlooking the fact that religion is of the heart and more or less of little value without "works." The new zealots entirely overlooked the unostentatious "giving" of such men as the noted gambler Byron Hames and his associates, who provided caskets and burial plots for the "fallen"; who never failed to feed a hungry man; and who provided clothing and food for the improvident's family.

When none of the Protestant ministers would help in a sinner's distress, except to deliver an anathema, you'd find such men as Father K. of the little south side Catholic Parish working with those awful men (such as Hames, Gleason and their group) to assuage the grief and the wants of those whom the Kansas reformers disdained to help. With this background, let's call out the fire department and live once again through that night of nights when it looked as though all homes and many people would be destroyed.

The time is approximately 11 P.M., on a windy night in March, about 1908. Up to this time reformers had not arrived in sufficient numbers to forever lay Old Town to rest (ultimately they did, but not yet). We good people at this time had the reformers outnumbered by a few votes.

Then came the fire. It started at Red M's (the red-headed Negro madam), or close thereby and because of the terrific wind, had shortly encircled the entire red-light section. Fortunately the fire department was at the corner of 26th Street and Cucharras, almost within a stone's throw of the raging fire. The wind literally scattered flaming embers over the entire city and most citizens were hosing their roofs with water to prevent further extension of the raging fire.

In spite of the necessity of saving their own homes, many citizens made their way to 26th Street, to witness at first hand the holocaust—many of the old-timers to help; some of the reformers to give thanks, perhaps that the notorious red-light area was doomed and its tinseled girls and painted madams homeless, injured or dead.

Jack Diamond of fire-fighting fame and locally known as a semiprofessional boxer, was a hose-man. He was doing valiantly in trying to smother the flames, but it looked hopeless.

Preacher B. was tempted and fell. He, too, could not resist the inner urge to see a red-light section in flames. Unlike rough-neck Jack Diamond, this eminent Divine was not present to help, but to watch prayerfully. Little did he apparently care about saving the bodies of the "fallen" from the flames; but his interest (although unrevealed) apparently lay in the future saving of the girls from the fire that's supposed to sear souls. One cannot surmise the emotions of a man at a time like this except by his deeds or words. The author had opportunity to observe the deeds of Jack Diamond and his worthy neighbors so intent on saving life and property. During the midst of the fire, when all looked hopeless, the author glanced at the preacher to see his reaction and heard him proclaim, "Thank God for this fire and the destruction of the red light district." The girls were shivering in scanty attire; some with blankets around them, watching what little they possessed going up in flames.

That, my friend, was too much, much too much for valiant Jack Diamond. In one fast pass, he turned the full force of the hose on Mr. Preacher and let him have it with fervency and power, if not with prayer. You can imagine what happened to the Rev. Mr. B. Within a matter of seconds he was a sheet of ice—"à la ice statue." It might have been a cruel thing to do—I'll leave that surmise to you, especially on a below-zero night—but I confess that in spite of the night's tragedy, here and there among my neighbors I could discern a spark of enjoyment. Needless to say, the Rev. Mr. B. hastily retreated to his cloistered sanctuary—possibly to pray, possibly to thaw out.

Not long thereafter Rev. B. quietly betook himself to parts distant, possibly thinking that his zeal might fare better elsewhere. Later other reformers finally completed Old Town's total annihilation. Out went the saloons, out went the few remaining Parlor Houses, and out went most of the town's business. The phrase Old Town so proudly hailed on its banner, "Old Town against the World," has passed like its red light section into oblivion. "So fades the Works of Man."

Oh, yes, you ask, what became of Jack Diamond? He later was killed doing his duty as brakeman on the Short Line Cripple Creek railroad. He made no great profession of faith, but in the old days you'd frequently see him in the presence of Father K. I rather think they are together somewhere, where fires are not of much concern. Possibly Father K. sold him a fire-escape, I wouldn't know; but I do know that Rev. B. wound up as a Living Ice Statue of the Great Fire of Old Town's Red Light section.

But all this was years later, and I am supposed to be telling about the times long ago when I was only five, and didn't know anything at all about such things. It was that year that the song "Chippy, Get Your Hair Cut, Hair Cut, Just Like Mine" came out. In those days a short haircut was the trade-mark of girls in the profession, but we children sang it and whistled it just as loudly as anyone else. We thought it was a lovely song.

Some time that fall our big new house on the hill north of town was finished; and when we moved into it, we really moved everything, even the little house we had lived in behind the café. Father set it up in our new back yard and used it for a barn. Some friends who followed us from Kansas led Nellie's colt Barney behind their wagon. Evidently the colt was too young to bring with us when we had left in the spring; but now we had him with us again, and he moved into the house that we had just vacated. I don't know whether or not he appreciated the honor, but I must tell you about my brother Burt's reaction to the fact that the house in which he had been born was now a stable.

Some years later, the Sunday-school teacher was telling Burt's class the story of Christmas. When she got to the place where Jesus was born in the stable, Burt's eyes flashed and he leaped to his feet.

"I was born in a stable too!" he blurted out.

He even brought troops of his little friends over to show them the stable in which he was born. Needless to say, I always considered his claims completely fraudulent.

The winter before we moved into our new house, I went a block beyond to the one-room stone school the Old Town then supported, and learned absolutely nothing. I distinctly recall the arithmetic classes. We were supposed to be doing simple sums, but I was under the impression that the teacher was playing a guessing game with us. Whenever I was given a problem, I would simply choose a number, any number, from one to ten. On those rare occasions when I guessed right, I felt like a modern gambler who has just called "Bingo!"

The school faced the Colorado Midland Railroad tracks, and we would listen for the trains to go by instead of paying attention to what the teacher was trying to tell us, so no wonder we didn't learn anything. We always carried a handful of pins to school. We would take two and carefully cross them, with the heads of the pins in one direction, and lay them on the track so that when the train passed over them they were mashed together in such a way as to form a pair of scissors, if the wheels did not pick them up and throw them to one side. If there happened to be a perfect pair of scissors, everyone claimed it, and a free-for-all ensued.

The next year we had a new eight-room brick school right in the center of the rapidly growing town, across the street from our stores. It was later known as the Old Bancroft School. But we were very proud of it then, and it was there that I learned that doing sums was not merely a mild form of entertainment or guesswork.

We had a lot of fun at school, though. There was a fence of horizontal iron pipes across the front from which we used to hang by our knees and perform other gymnastic feats. One noon period a group of us were hanging quietly from the top pipe when we were suddenly regaled with a most hilarious sight. A determined-looking cow came bawling and running down the middle of the street just as fast as she could go. There was a rope around her neck, and tied to the rope at the other end was a man. He was leaning back on the rope and taking long strides. He would seem to be hovering in the air an interminable time before he would land on one heel in a flurry of dust, then into the air he would go to land on the other heel. He was somewhat bowlegged, and that made it all the funnier. We laughed until the tears ran down our cheeks. I could hardly wait to get home and tell the folks what had happened in school that day.

"You should have seen the funniest thing!" I shouted to Mother, as I burst into the door that evening. "A cow ran away with a man right down the middle of the avenue in front of the school."

"Hush!" Mother whispered, clapping her hand over my mouth, as she glanced over her shoulder toward the bedroom door. "That was your father!"

And, indeed, it was Father. He was in bed for a week with a wrenched back. But we had the cow. She shared our old house with Barney when she was not out on the huge meadow that stretched all the way between Colorado City and Colorado Springs. My poor sister Myrtie spent most of her adolescent years, I think, out on the meadow looking for that cow.

As usual, when the more restless members of a family take a step, others soon follow. Our family was no exception, and that spring Father's sister and her husband and baby, the Charley Taylors, arrived. Uncle Charley opened a dry-goods store a block east of Father's café, and continued in business there for many years. Then Grandmother Hunt and Father's unmarried sister, Aunt Amelia, came. Grandmother Hunt had continued to operate the hotel at Carbondale until she found a buyer. Now they opened a grocery store right across the street from the school and lived in a couple of rooms back of the store. At that time our family, and the druggist and his family, the McIntoshes, had the distinction of being the only business people in town who were not operating a saloon or gambling place.

Anyway, whenever things would get dull, we of the second-grade set used to cross the street to Grandmother Hunt's store and beg cracked eggs and soft tomatoes to throw at the bobbed-tail horses the English of Colorado Springs used to ride and drive tandem to and from Manitou. At that time Colorado Springs was practically a British colony, and anything we could do to detract from their dignity we considered most laudable, if not downright patriotic. Besides, there is probably nothing more completely satisfying than the experience of hitting a solid object squarely with an overripe tomato. And we spent many an enjoyable afternoon throwing our eggs and tomatoes at the English and their ridiculous horses. Even when we missed, it was most amusing to hear them shout at us in their curious accent. And speaking of accents, it seems strange to me now that I never realized that Grandmother Hunt herself was as English as the Tower of London.

One day she asked us what we did with all the cracked eggs and old tomatoes she gave us. In her innocence, I suppose she thought we took them home and ate them. And in my innocence, I gaily told her the truth, half expecting that she might like to come out and join in the fun. She didn't.

"So!" she said, drawing herself up in freezing dignity. "You throw them at my countrymen. I shall tell your father."

That was the only time in my life I ever saw Grandmother Hunt angry, and I never cared to make her angry again. What's more, she did tell Father, too, and that was the end of my second and last experiment in racial relations.

It was sometime that year that an epidemic of smallpox in a very virulent form broke out in the town, and a great many died of it. All the women and children in our family came to live with us, and we were isolated—a sort of quarantine in reverse. The men stayed at the stores and attended to their various businesses. We were all vaccinated, but a cousin and I were the only ones who had any reaction from the inoculation. I remember that we were too sick to play for several days. Fortunately, none of the family contracted the disease, and the whole affair turned out to be a sort of house party.

We did need a curfew to keep the children off the streets at night. Of course, there were no movies, and when a rare show passed our way, like *Uncle Tom's Cabin,* we might go with some older member of the family. Since we had no theater, we would go to the matinee at Colorado Springs; and we entertained ourselves at home. Mother allowed us to make trains of the kitchen chairs. We even had one pullman—two chairs facing and the couch pillows and a shawl to make a bed for the little one, Neva, our little sister, and the last of ten children. After much discussion she was named for the other little Neva who lived only a short time. Mother liked the name very much. Sometimes we popped corn and on rare occasions made pop-corn balls; but when Father came home from the store early, we played cards. Mother had never seen a deck of cards until she was married. They were strictly taboo in her and her relatives' homes, but my father's people were not farmers; they were of the business world, and they all played cards. Grandmother Hunt watched the games and was very much interested, but at one time Grandfather Hunt had criticized a play she made, and she vowed she would never play another game of cards. And being a most determined person, she never did.

Of course, we did not play for anything, and only played in the evening when Father was at home. He would get the cards out of a little drawer under the clock shelf; and Mother would say, "Why don't you let them win some time? They go to bed crying every time you play."

And he would answer, "I give no quarter; and until they learn the game, I will beat them every time." And he did, until we finally learned the game—it was casino. Later, when we moved to Victor, the game was "solo," sometimes called "sluff." We all learned to play it—he taught us; it was the gambling game next to poker. We played it with poker chips, and I mean *played* it, even to the youngest, Neva. That was the one game to which Mother objected, because sometimes one game lasted hours. The bidding really upset her—"frog," "little one," and "big one" (solos). She said it might be all right for a saloon but not a home. It is still played at clubs, but very few women play it. I have always been glad Father taught it to us. Now my son Earl says he can always take all my chips at sluff, and almost always he does. Mother did in later years play six-handed euchre, and she played a good game too.

The most colorful character in Old Town was Byron Haymes, known as the Gambling King. He always wore a full-dress suit and a tall, black silk hat, and carried a gold-headed cane. He didn't need a bouncer. My uncle, who was in the dry-goods business, and Byron, who was in the "wet goods" business (he operated a saloon and gambling house), were associated in many business deals. At that time Byron was quite wealthy and at the top of his career; he was known for his many charities and was highly respected. A working man once came in and gambled and lost his entire paycheck. Byron met him as he was leaving and returned it to him, saying, "Do not come in here any more; you can't afford to lose." (There are many kinds of gamblers— the professional, the gentleman, and the tinhorn-cheap, making a meager living.)

His wife was a very pretty, small woman with dark hair and eyes. He bought her what was known as a trap, a fancy light carriage with rubberlike tire rims on the wheels. She drove a matched team of spirited black horses and was really something, with a large hat with a huge black ostrich feather on it. Everyone stopped to look when she whizzed by.

In the course of time all things change; and what with depressions and the opening of the gold camp and mostly when Prohibition ruined the liquor business, things went from bad to worse. Byron's building stood idle, and finally was sold for taxes; his wife and only son died, and he was alone. In desperation he washed dishes in a café in Denver for his meals and a place to sleep.

One day, many years later, I went to my uncle's store and saw a tall, shabby man. He was clad in a long linen duster that came nearly to his ankles. He looked familiar and I found it was really Byron Haymes. His new job was store detective, an entirely new and unneeded service; and true to Uncle's reputation for hospitality, he invited him to dinner. He stayed nine months, until he became so ill he was taken to Denver, I assume to a hospital. He died soon afterward, mourned and missed by few.

In the summer we used to look forward all week to the Sunday outing. There were many beautiful spots for our picnics, and at that early date our population was so small that we could choose many a now-famous spot and have it all to ourselves. We had a little crowd of our own composed of a neighbor's family and ours; and when, with our lunch baskets and coffee pot, we were loaded into our two-seated buggy and they in their light spring wagon, we were sufficient unto ourselves. We chose shady spots by running streams, from which we had water for drinking and cooking, and also for the horses. Indeed, the horses seemed to appreciate outings almost as much as we did; they took long drinks of the cold, running water and enjoyed the lush green grass and freedom.

Mother always wanted to leave a little early, as Barney would all but run away to get home to his evening meal of oats. We were always the first ones home; the later we left, the faster Barney would go.

Four spots I remember best. One was the Garden of the Gods. Actually we didn't like it too well, for it had no stream in which we could play. Another was Bear Creek Canyon; it had a beautiful stream and shade and was closer than the other spots. But our favorites were Manitou and South Cheyenne Canyon.

For the Manitou outing we had to be a little better dressed than for the others, but it had its compensations. There were Fountain Creek and the pretty picnic spots, but the main attraction was the lemonade we made of the iron water; it was bubbly and bitey and so cold we did not need ice for it. The iron spring at that time was more popular than any other in the locality. It was about two miles up a narrow curved road that turned left from the center of the town of Manitou, and was dotted with little curio shops along the way. And at the pavilion near the spring, we could buy hot buttered popcorn and salt-water taffy. We always enjoyed the day there.

Manitou water was known all over the country as the very finest bottled soda water; there was the plain soda and the finest ginger ale anyone ever drank. It was special, as the bottling company bought the ginger root and had their own formula. One drawback was the bottles that were shipped there, as they were quite expensive. So an up-to-date glass factory was built on South Twenty-sixth Street. There they made not only the bottles, but many other glass articles from the waste glass. Then there were large chunks of blue glass the citizens gathered for door stops and paperweights; and if a young lady was fortunate in having a beau who was a glass blower, the walls of her home were adorned with beautiful glass canes, made in many artistic designs and fastened on the walls with huge bows of ribbon. It was one of the very few industries, and it was a real calamity when the factory burned down one windy night and was never rebuilt.

But the best spot of all was Cheyenne Canyon, with its beautiful Seven Falls. It had only one drawback: even at that early time there was a toll gate; and we were quite a crowd. The small children were admitted free and the older ones had to pay half fare, but there were always at least eight adults with us, so we weren't able to go there as often as if there had been no toll. The canyon was a fairy paradise of superb scenery. It still is, but there was more water in the stream at that time, and the falls were spectacularly beautiful. The pine trees were unusually large and whispery and fragrant, and in the spring the air was pleasantly pungent with the bitter-sweet aroma of choke cherries. Later, the cherries themselves were just as bitter. I can remember the times when we children's mouths were so puckered from eating them that all the picnic food tasted the same.

And there was the incense of the wild roses, and a shrub that in season bore a large, single white blossom almost as fragrant as the wild rose itself. Later, it produced a red berry made up almost entirely of small hard seeds with almost no flavor.

The two most beautiful flowers grew only in the shade. One was the columbine, now the state flower. The cultivated variety comes in many shades, with both double and single blooms, but the wild columbine is in a class all by itself. The five outside petals are a deep lavender; inside is a smaller cup-shaped bloom composed of five white petals. And in the very center are numerous yellow stamens. Even at that time they were not too plentiful, and to find them required a great deal of climbing and searching. But when we found them swaying on their long, graceful stems, with all the delicate scent of the woods distilled in their exquisite chalices, we knew they were worth the effort.

Then there was the rare lady's-slipper, colored like an orchid and shaped like a tiny slipper. We were delighted when we discovered a cluster of these in the most shaded damp spots.

The chief attraction was the rickety-looking stairs, with a none-too-secure hand rail on one side, rising straight up the side of the canyon almost directly over the cascading Seven Falls. From the top of the stairs the view was magnificent. Looking northeast, we could clearly see the new little town of Colorado Springs; and all about us on the plateau stretched the beautiful wild forest, teeming with flowers, and the bright-colored birds, and the little chipmunks and squirrels. Through the pines a little path led to the grave of Helen Hunt Jackson, a mound piled high with stones in the center of a small clearing. The stones were mostly decomposed granite that sparkled in the sunshine, and that we thought might be gold. In these tranquil surroundings she had been inspired to write the story of the Indian maiden Ramona. Here she would bring her notebook and the light lunch she would share with the blue jays, the cardinals, the raucous camp robbers, and the chipmunks that became so tame they would eat from her hand, while the numer-

ous little birds scolded her and begged for crumbs. Here to
the music of the waterfall and whispering pine, she had written
her nature-inspired story. And here in death she then lay
beneath the mound, as she had requested. We had but few
tourists then, and fewer still who braved the rickety steps over
the falls; they were asked to add a rock to her grave, and the
mound grew. But later the path grew wider and the mound
became smaller, as more and more visitors came to the grave.
Apparently they wished to take away with them more than a
memory. With the casket almost laid bare, friends and relatives
were repeatedly obliged to carry in more rocks, until finally the
family moved her to their plot in Evergreen Cemetery in Colorado Springs, where she now lies beneath a protecting black
marble slab. Around her the grass is a green carpet and the
roses bloom in profusion. I have always felt it a pity that she
could not have been left in the spot she loved on the wild
mountainside, so hauntingly beautiful that only God could have
made it.

Little did we know that all these happy times were about
to come to an end, for that summer, 1892, as soon as school was
out, Mother decided to take us on a trip to Wisconsin. It was
a happy and memorable summer, and the last one we spent at
Grandpap and Grandmother Doll's home. On our way back to
Colorado, we stopped off at Carbondale, near the little town in
Kansas where I was born, and visited the graves of my five little
brothers and sisters. We also went to the hotel that Grandmother
Hunt had owned when we lived there. It was not as large as
I had remembered, but it was still quite large. It had two
stories and all of Grandmother Hunt's children, except Father,
had lived there with her. There was Aunt Tillie, Father's oldest
sister, and her husband Uncle Grant and their two children,
Tillie and Sam; then there was Uncle Billy, and Aunt Amelia,
whom we called our "old maid" aunt, and their younger sister
Della. I can recall how, as very little children, we loved to go
to Grandmother's hotel. Our house was small, and we were not
allowed to play running games indoors, but in the hotel we

played hide-and-seek both upstairs and down, and no one objected.

When we came home that fall, rumors were rife about the fabulous gold strikes being made in the Cripple Creek district, and since business in Colorado City had gone into a slump and my father was considering a move of some kind, the thought of a booming mining camp was most alluring to him. So another move was in the offing.

CHAPTER VI

VICTOR

The leaves are fading and falling,
　The winds are rough and wild,
The birds have ceased their calling,
　But let me tell you, my child,
That day by day as it closes,
　And they darker and colder grow,
The roots of the bright red roses,
　Are kept alive in the snow.

There must be rough, cold weather,
　And winds and rains so wild;
Not all good things together
　Come us here, my child.
So when some bright joy loses
Its beauteous summer glow,
Think how the roots of the roses
Are kept alive in the snow.

ALICE CARY

　This beautiful poem might have been in one of our readers at school; I always felt it reflected the hope in the hearts of the pioneers. When the flame of hope burned low, there was always a tiny spark that could be fanned to burn brightly again.

　It was six years since we had arrived in Colorado City. Father had built six houses, including the little two-room one back of the café that was moved and later used as a barn. Each one was larger and better than the preceding one, and six times, in spite of her protests, Mother had moved.

　He had been in four different businesses, the meat market,

the café, a gent's clothing store, and now he had a new-and-used furniture store.

While we had much more than when we had arrived in the camp wagon, business was slow, and he was discouraged and considering another location. In the fall of 1892 he was excavating for another house higher up on the hill, although Mother had declared positively that she would not move again. About this time rumors began to be circulated about the fabulous gold strike in Cripple Creek, and Father went there to investigate. When he returned, he already had an option on a lot in Victor and had decided that *that* was where we were going to move. He went up a time or two between then and Christmas to arrange details; and right after Christmas, in 1893, he went to erect the buildings for his secondhand furniture store and living quarters for us in the rear, while Mother stayed at home with the children, who were still in school. Myrtie had married a young man from Old Town and was now living in her own home, leaving me the oldest of the children at home. I was then eleven, and Mother had to depend more on me; for although Myrtie had left, there were still four of us children at home. Neva, our baby sister, had been born just about the time Myrtie was married.

Our home would have to be sold, of course, as the money was needed for the new venture. Our new-and-used-furniture business in Colorado City was now closed, as Father intended to move the entire stock to the new location. He made arrangements with "Old Tom," a simple, friendly old fellow who lived in a shack just below us, to do the chores, which included the care of Barney, our beloved horse. He was supposed to water him out of a pail at the hydrant; instead he led him down to the irrigation ditch, which was no doubt easier, but Barney refused to drink ditch water. So he came to the house and told Mother that he didn't blame him: "That water ain't fit for a man to drink, let alone a horse."

He also had a hobby of keeping pet rats—big white ones— and he wanted to give us children a pair. But Mother said, "No rats." He did, however, give us a pair, and we smuggled

them upstairs. We would slip food from the table into our
pockets to carry up to them, but Mother finally caught us in the
act. The rats were very tame and not hard to catch, and it was
easy to carry them back to Tom.

When school was out, May 24, 1893, to be exact, Father
came for us. He hired a man who had a large wagon and a
heavy team of horses to move the furniture from the store and
also the household furniture, part of which would go into the
store, as we would not need all of it in our two little rooms
at the rear. We could hardly wait to get started. The colt
Barney was now seven years old, gentle and willing to pull the
two-seated buggy, which was heavily loaded with our personal
belongings, besides the six of us.

The road was beautiful, more or less a trail known as the
Stage Road, as it was the shortest route to the gold camp; but
it was quite steep, at least the first part of it, which wound
around Cheyenne Mountain, where we had picnicked many
Sundays in the past, and climbed up Seven Falls. The day was
perfect. Father tied the reins around the whip, and Barney
went on ahead, stopping for a breathing spell now and then.
When he reached the top, he would kick up his heels and look
back at us, and whinney. He always waited for us, for we all
walked up the steepest hills.

It was evening when we came in sight of the first mining
activity on Bull Hill. There was a miners' strike on at the time.
The men were asking for an eight-hour, three-dollar day, which
they deserved and finally won the following year. They had
pickets posted, and we were stopped and searched for firearms.
They asked for the horse to use for picket duty that night; but
since it was apparent he was very tired after the forty-mile trip,
they let him rest that night, but used him many nights afterward.

The Strong Mine had been blown up May 25, 1893, but at
the time Father did not know about it. Mr. McDonold, the
superintendent, and two miners were in the mine at the time,
but were uninjured. Stratton had been favorable to the strikers
up to this time, but was very angry when they now closed
his mine.

After we were stopped at the foot of Bull Hill, and Mother was over her nervousness, my father told us there was a little town on top of the mountain we had just passed. It was called Altman, and was the highest incorporated city in the world. He said it was a small town consisting of a saloon, several grocery stores, a schoolhouse, several boardinghouses, and quite a few shacks where the miners batched or had their families. He said the striking miners had a fort overlooking all the country around, including the road we were traveling, as it was the main entrance to Victor and several smaller settlements. He said it was reported there was a cannon installed on top of the roughly built fort, and we could see it if we looked back. While we did not know much about forts, we could see something at the very top that looked like a stove pipe, and that, Father said, was a cannon. Where the strikers had found it, or how they had gotten it up there, no one knew.

We found out later that what looked like a stove pipe really was several lengths of stove pipe camouflaged in such a way that it looked like a cannon. He told us the men guarding the fort were striking miners, and they had guns and dynamite to blow up anyone or anything that hindered their cause. He said there were seven or eight hundred armed men at the fort.

Father's store had been hurriedly put up, or thrown together, as they said. It was a long two-story frame building. The rooms upstairs were rented, with the restaurant, which occupied a little less than half, downstairs. There was space for a bedroom in the rear of it; and in the space back of our side was the kitchen, living room, and dining room, all in one. It was close quarters. We were spoiled. We had been living in good houses for some time.

There was also a very small room between the kitchen and the furniture store. This was the undertaking room. Caskets were piled at one end, and there was a cot for me at the other. When a corpse was brought in, my cot was folded up and put in the store during the day. At night the corpse and I exchanged bed space. The first few nights, I'll admit, I didn't like the idea of being so close to the dead, even with a closed door between us; but they say you can get used to anything, even being hanged. So in due time I didn't mind, and Father said not to be afraid of the dead, but to look out for the living.

Many strange things happen in the undertaking business. A doctor and surgeon engaged a housekeeper, and in due time she came to buy a lot in the cemetery; she really wanted to rent one, but that was not possible. She said her mother was being shipped, that she was not sure how long she might stay in the locality, and that she always moved her everywhere she went. In due course the body arrived and was properly buried. Soon afterward it was disinterred and followed her daughter to her new address.

An undertaking company, Hallett & Baker, from Colorado Springs, had established their business in Cripple Creek, about seven miles from Victor, where we were located, and a branch of the company was started in our building. My father was not an undertaker or licensed embalmer, so a member of the Cripple Creek branch would come over and embalm the bodies if they were to be shipped. Father helped and learned fast, and in a short time he went to Denver, where he passed the State Board examination and became a fullfledged undertaker. However, we continued for several years with the company.

And here we had our second deck. It wasn't much to brag about. It was built a little on the order of the mezzanine floors they have now in big department stores. It was just a wide shelf built across about one-fourth of one side of our store, and had no fancy elevator, just rough steps; and here the old broken furniture that could be bought was mended and painted and sold before it could even dry.

The camp was growing rapidly. Tiny car-roofed shacks sprang up overnight, and there was little furniture to be had. The demand was much greater than the supply.

We children were quite disappointed, the first few weeks. It rained constantly, and was cold. We looked longingly at the beautiful country that began right in our back yard. The grass was green and the quaking aspen trees had put out their first tender leaves. Tall, dark pines grew between them, and the wildflowers were beginning to bloom. Saucy chipmunks played around our door, and we could hardly wait to get outside and make figure-four traps to catch them. This we did as soon as we could get out, and lined cages up against the stage barn that was built on the back of our lot. My, how those pretty, striped little things could bite! And they gnawed themselves out almost as fast as we put them in the wooden-box cages.

There was no laundry in Victor. One afternoon when the passenger train from Florence pulled into the station, a very businesslike Chinese got off. All the luggage he seemed to have was a sort of bundle. He found a little one-room shack and took possession. He created quite a sensation, and soon had callers. The committee inquired what his business in town might be. He pointed to the little rough board sign over the door, which he must have had in his bundle when he arrived. It said SING LEE LAUNDRY. In no time at all he was all packed up and escorted down the narrow-gauge railroad track, and bid a fond and hurried adieu. Exit Chinaman.

I had played most of my life with boys, and rode that mean ginny when she would let me on her back, so I was a pretty good rider. However, I wanted more than anything else to ride the bell horse that led the four horses that hauled the stage six days a week. She had a bell fastened to her collar and was really fast. She might have been part bronco. Her disposition was none too good, but I tried to make friends with her and brought her cookies and piece of apple. She accepted my gifts with her ears laid back and showing the whites of her eyes.

It was a red-letter day when my parents allowed me to go to Cripple Creek on that stage. Charlie, the driver, came to the door and asked if I could ride on the box seat on top of the old stage with him next day. When they agreed, I was so excited I was the first one up and ready to go, long before the stage was ready to leave. The store and barn was on Fourth Street, about half a block south of Victor Avenue. The first stop would be on this corner, and then out Victor Avenue.

There were two small settlements between Victor and Cripple Creek. The first was Elkton, just a small cabin or two, since the Elkton mine had just been discovered. The other was Anaconda, perhaps a little larger place. Charlie said he would sometimes pick up a passenger or two at one of these places. He also carried part of the mail. That day the stage was full and a man also sat with us on the box seat.

In all my wildest dreams I had never imagined anything so thrilling as that ride. Charlie had a long whip, and while he would crack it and shout at the horses, he really did not use it otherwise. He didn't need to—those horses went their best, and the old stage bumped over the rough new road. If there were any tenderfeet inside that stage, they must have been scared and plenty shaken up.

It was only seven miles to Cripple Creek, and the time went all too fast. I had a quarter for my lunch, and while Charlie attended to the business for the return trip at two o'clock, I ate my lunch and felt grown-up enough to walk into a café alone. There was a sign on the window announcing bear steak as the specialty of the day. So that is what I had for my lunch, but I was disappointed, because it was greasy and stringy and tough. Then I walked up one side and down the other of Bennett Avenue, the only main street, and looked in the store windows. I also called on Father's partner, Mr. Hallett. The time passed quickly. The ride home was just as thrilling, and I talked about it for many days. I wonder why my brother Gil didn't ask to go, but he didn't seem much impressed.

At this time I was the tomboy of the family. It was on this ride I asked Charlie if I could ride the bell horse some Sunday. He said, "Sure, if you can stick on." He also said he didn't know whether she had ever had a saddle on her back. Of course, when we had the ginny, we rode her bareback with only a bridle. My parents didn't seem to have any doubts about my being able to ride, but they did say she needed to rest that day. When I reminded them of the many miles a day our horses had traveled hauling loads, I didn't think the seven miles to Cripple Creek and back was too much of a trip. The bell horse agreed with my folks that she didn't want to be ridden, and she sure didn't like me—perhaps it was my petticoats. But except for the Sunday we all went to Cripple Creek and panned for gold, I rode her every Sunday.

The first Sunday we found she either had never had a saddle on her back or had forgotten it. Charlie was a real horseman, and with a little help from one of the stablemen, he got her bridle on and the saddle firmly girthed. Then he got on her. She bucked some but not as bad as that ginny could buck. I wasn't afraid to ride her. Charlie rode her around the block, and then he helped me on her, much to her disgust, and handed me a riding whip.

"Let her know you are the boss," he said. I thought I was, but I soon found out I was not. We, the horse and I, went east on Victor Avenue at a pretty fast gallop, then north past the newly discovered Stratton mine and off the main road past the pump house, where the McKenzies lived. We had recently met them. Mr. McKenzie was the engineer. We stopped there a few minutes and offered Bell a drink, but she was too mad to drink. I didn't get off for fear I couldn't get on again.

Next we came to Goldfield, at that time a very small settlement of cabins and little two- or three-room houses. There were no fences, but each back yard had its clothes line. I didn't see the clothes line, but Bell did. She took the bit firmly in her teeth; and before we hit the first one, I barely had time to duck and cling to her neck. Some were lower than others, and she nearly brushed me off. The whip was no good as she had things well under control. I wondered if she would turn and come back under them again, but she made for the main road that went up Bull Hill.

There was another small settlement, Independence. The road went through the one street, so we didn't hit the back yards. I was tempted to go on to the top of Bull Hill where the union held fort and guarded the road we had taken when we came to Victor, but I was afraid they might want to use Bell for picket duty as they had our horse.

So we went back down the road, and she didn't try to go through Goldfield and the clothes lines on the way home. When I got back and told Charlie what she had tried to do, he said he would go along someday and I could ride another horse; and he bet she wouldn't try to brush him off. I rode her many Sundays that summer, and every time she tried to get rid of me. It became a sort of game. I didn't want to ride another horse, so Charlie never rode with me. Besides, I was afraid he would be too rough on her, and I didn't want her hurt. I liked her.

There is an undercurrent of excitement in a boom town, and Victor was no exception. While I was young at the time, I shared with many of my elders the thought and hope that I could walk along the trails and pick up hunks of gold. The nearest I ever came to it was discovering a pretty blue streak of rock that glittered in the sunlight. I took a small piece of it home, and found it was sylvanite. When I went back for more, someone had taken all of it out. It was a small pocket. Since it was just below what later became the famous Ajax mine, which produced millions, it could have been an outcropping of that rich vein.

This wild dream of finding gold was not altogether an illusion, as some of the most fabulous producing mines were discovered by poor men at the grass roots. The Independence, for instance, was discovered by a carpenter, Mr. Stratton, who knew nothing about minerals. But he certainly knew the needs of the poor and aged, as the millions that came out of that mine have been put to lasting use for good. He built what is known as the Myron Stratton Home in Colorado Springs, many beautiful, comfortable buildings surrounded by a natural park, where the poor and aged not only find a refuge, but every modern luxury, maintained by the clean wealth produced by that one mine, a lasting monument to that generous man and dedicated to the memory of his father, Myron Stratton.

The home later added children's buildings, where orphans and children from broken homes were not only cared for, but loved and educated. Many fine men and women grew up in Stratton Home.

An inscription on his beautiful monument in Evergreen Cemetery reads: IT IS NOT ENOUGH TO HELP THE FEEBLE UP—

BUT TO SUPPORT HIM AFTER. On Memorial Day, children from the home scatter on the grave the wildflowers he loved.

One of the regrettable mistakes that Mr. Stratton made was leaving almost his entire estate to the building and maintenance of the Myron Stratton Home. At that time El Paso County included the Cripple Creek district, and it was chiefly for the benefit of the residents of the area from which he derived his wealth that he wished to establish the home. Shortly after his death, the county was divided, and the western part became Teller County, but since the will specified that to participate in the benefits of the home the applicants must be resident of El Paso County for the preceding fifteen years, this excluded Teller County residents.

In contrast to Mr. Stratton's generosity, I remember an incident that took place in a Sunday-school class in the little church in Victor. One of the wealthiest men in the community was a member of the class, and one morning I saw him put a quarter into the collection plate and take out four nickels in change.

One Sunday soon after we were settled, and the rains were over, we drove Barney to Cripple Creek, about seven miles from Victor. This was the place where the gold excitement really started. It was not the same as the gold discovered in veins of rock, but was found in the sand along a tiny stream so crooked it was called Cripple Creek, after which the town was named. Here on both sides of the creek, specified distances apart, men had hurriedly set up what they called cradles, rudely built affairs, to rock and wash the sand and dirt away and leave only the shiny gold nuggets in the pan or trough. Two men whom my folks had known in Kansas had a spot on the bank. One was an old man, Jack Peacock, a queer little hunchback fellow with a pointed beard. The other was a very tall man, more than six feet six, called Shorty George. They were a queer couple but real buddies, and had prospected together for many years. It was truly marvelous to see the shovelful of dirt turn into bright golden pebbles, and they let us each wash a pan. The little pill bottle full of gold nuggets was my prized possession for a long time, until we decided to combine our treasures into one nugget, and had a pin made with Mother's initials on it for her birthday. I wonder where that is now?

That summer, a temporary school building was hastily built. As I remember, it was a long, low building with what they called a car roof, which was a roof just like the roofs used on box cars. It was slightly rounded and higher in the middle, and slanted to the front and back to drain off the rain or melting snow. It was made of corrugated iron; and when it hailed, which it often does in that altitude, the noise was terrific, and we could hardly hear ourselves think. There were six rooms about fourteen by sixteen feet in size. Each room had regular desks and seats, a round potbellied stove, a blackboard, a globe of the world, a large dictionary on a rack, and a flat-top desk and swivel chair for the teacher.

On a small bench in each room was a pail of water. These were filled by the janitor twice daily from a large barrel in the service room, which in turn was filled daily by tank-wagon service. The water came from a spring, and was the only water supply in the district at the time. There were two long-handled dippers in each pail. We all drank out of the same dippers, but I can not remember any epidemics of colds or grippe, as it was called at that time.

There was a narrow porch all along the front of the building, and wooden steps up to it for entering each room. With only one window in front and one in the back it did not make for very good lighting. Neither did the big round stove give out the right kind of heat; those who sat close roasted and the ones in the far corners were cold.

This building was the grade school. A combined high school and grade school was built the next year. I was in the seventh grade, but since there were fewer seventh- and eighth-graders, we occupied the same room. The distance to school was quite far for the first- and second-graders to walk, especially in blizzards and bad weather, so those two grades also occupied one room. This schoolhouse was the only one, except the one built that same summer in Cripple Creek, so the pupils came from the little settlements like Altman, Independence, Goldfield, and Elkton. Most of them brought their lunches. The school was built on quite a large plot of ground; it must have been an entire square block, between Second and Third streets. I think it was leased for that one year only. The next year, when the school building was moved or torn down, some of the better homes were built on that location, also the Presbyterian Church.

It was really the only level spot in Victor, and the only place where a large group of children could play. Our room had a baseball team, and we would get so interested in our game that we either would not hear the bell at the end of the fifteen-minute recess, or ignored it. The younger children would go in, and finally Professor Pruitt would come down. If the inning was about over, and interesting, he would wait for us, and warn us about the next time. We all liked him. There were several big boys in the class, perhaps sixteen years of age, but there was never any trouble. Mr. Pruitt was the principal of the school, but we called him "the professor."

Few teachers matched his method of teaching spelling. Every morning he brought the Denver *Post*, which came in on the stage from Colorado Springs. He would sit in the swivel chair, put his feet on the desk, light his large cigar, and our spelling lesson lasted as long as the cigar. He gave us words out of the paper, and would occasionally read us a short article he thought would be of interest to us. We would write down the words as they sounded to us; and at the end of the session he would spell them correctly. Since thirty of us could not use the large dictionary fast enough, he would give us the meaning of the words. We would correct our own papers, after which we had a study period; then he would give us the words again and would correct and grade our papers. It was fun, and we learned to spell many words that we would not have encountered in regular spelling books, and also learned the meaning of them.

The next year the new schoolhouse was ready, and Professor Pruitt went into the real estate business. The new principal was Mr. J. P. Wright. He also taught the eighth and ninth grades, which occupied one room and were the classes that continued through high school.

The first morning he made a short speech, and at the close told us his slogan: "I would rather be Wright than President." He was a good teacher and we all liked him very much.

The school was a two-story frame structure and was more modern than the temporary one. We had a furnace, but still no running water. The teacher across the hall taught the sixth and seventh grades. We thought she was very old, an old maid; now I would say she was perhaps between forty and forty-five. Her name was Bolby and we called her "Bawl Baby," but not when she was liable to overhear us, of course.

The first- and second-graders, who were in one room, had a teacher by the name of Miss Etta Myers. She had been my second-grade teacher in Colorado City, and she was a very fine teacher. Later for a short time she was married to Mr. Rasmussen, and continued to teach in Victor schools several years.

We had what we called a literary club. It met the last session Friday afternoons once a month. Sometimes someone would read a short story or an article from some magazine, but always there were two or three who recited the same poem. One was especially popular, Pearl Aspey's recitation of "Laska." Pearl was a pretty little slim blond girl, and we always had to coax her to recite. She would say all she knew was the same one, and we heard it many times; but we would insist and she would tell us in a very dramatic way in poetry about the stampede of the cattle in Texas, down on the Rio Grande, how the only hope was to quickly get off your horse and shoot it, then lie flat on the ground as close to it as possible, and how the rider and his girl companion Laska did this, and at the last moment, before the thundering herd passed over them, she protected him with her own body. And after the herd had passed, Laska was dead. We would listen spellbound, always knowing how it would end, but ever with the hope it would end differently.

The third year after the new school was built, the school decided to have a public program to raise money for some books we needed. The city of Victor had built a public hall called the Armory. It had been used to store arms and ammunition during the strike, but for such a good cause we had it rent free for one evening. There was an oration contest and I was one of the orators. My subject was Lincoln. The hall was large and filled to capacity with our families and friends. I remember very clearly the opening lines of my oration—a teacher had helped me and I thought they were very good. They were "As the scroll revealing the past is unfolded to our view, written thereon are the names of men who have become famous." Just when I had concluded this impressive opening, I looked over the large audience and had stage fright and forgot the next paragraph. Luckily for me, at that instant there was a disturbance in the rear of the hall, and nearly everyone stood up. There was so much noise and confusion that no one noticed that I was not continuing my speech. When quiet and order was restored, I remembered my lines and concluded. I was awarded first prize, an enlarged tinted picture of the schoolhouse, teachers, and pupils. We raised so much more money than we needed that the club voted to have my picture framed. I still have it and often look at it, but there are only a few in the picture I remember by name.

At the close of my senior year, Mr. and Mrs. Wright moved to Denver, where he had a public office in the Court House; and a new brick high school was built on West Victor Avenue. A Mr. Whitmore was the new principal.

CHAPTER VII

MOVING DAYS

Since moving seemed to be the natural thing to do every spring, reasons why we should move were being discussed and argued over. As usual, Mother said she wouldn't move; and as usual, when the time came, we moved. The furniture business had outgrown the storeroom, and most assuredly the undertaking business had outgrown my bedroom. So when the building a couple of blocks north on the other side of the street was completed, we rented it temporarily, and moved. This time the furniture business really occupied the deck, and we lived underneath at the back. One side was used for furniture and the other side, a separate room, was used for our undertaking, as we needed space to hold funeral services. It was built on the side of the mountain facing the narrow-gauge Florence and Cripple Creek Railroad. Rough stairs led down to where we now had four rooms: two bedrooms, a kitchen and dining room combined, and a living room—all very small. The back part of the deck had a railing across it, but was left open so we could hear the telephone. It seemed to ring too often. Inadequate housing and the cold weather caused a great many deaths from pneumonia, but they were nothing compared to the accidents in the mines. Now we had two horse-drawn hearses, one black and one white, and they seemed to be in use every day.

Following a brawl in which two men had been killed and a dance-hall woman had committed suicide, a cop who was a match for the toughest of them arrested the two ringleaders and attempted to lock them up in the Victor jail. But a mob had gathered and prevented him from jailing them. Knowing it was nearly time for the Florence and Cripple Creek train to arrive, he rushed his prisoners to the depot. They were cuffed together and one was handcuffed to him. The mob followed them. We could see the crowd from our window, and saw the engineer

forced at gun point to hold the train while the mob attempted
to uncouple the car in which the prisoners were taken to the
Cripple Creek jail. The officer fired several shots to frighten
the mob. No one was injured and the train pulled out, but only
to be met by another mob in Elkton, a small settlement about
three miles from Victor. This mob entered the car, but using
the prisoners as a shield, the officer shot into the group, killing
a man named Lumley, before the train pulled out. He finally
reached Cripple Creek with his prisoners. Lumley, who was
standing at the entrance to the car when he was shot, fell off
the back platform, and was left there until the coroner arrived,
who then called the undertaker. It seemed only a matter of
minutes after we saw the train pull out until there was a phone
call, and Father left with the Black Maria for the scene, and soon
returned with the corpse.

A huge crowd gathered in the store and undertaking rooms;
there were threats and loud talking far into the night. There
was a board sidewalk in front of the building, and a guard
paced up and down all night. We could hear the measured
beat of his boots plainly in the living room below.

The man was dead. I could never understand why there
had to be a guard stationed there. A large motley crowd attended the funeral, but there were no violent demonstrations.

The claim jumper was a citizen known by all the vile names
commonly applied to such characters, and there were a great
many of them. All the mines were acquired by filing claims on
them; the entire sides of the mountains in and around the district
are honeycombed with prospect holes today. The prospector
could drive his stake and claim a certain number of feet in each
direction. Then, since the county courthouse was in El Paso
County, in Colorado Springs, he would rush down and file his
claim. Then he had five years to prove his claim before he
received a title to it. The law required that he work the claim.
He could do all the assessment work in one year, or a specified
number of feet each year for five years. While he had been
staking the claim and writing his claim on it, he might be
observed by a claim jumper, who would move in as soon as

he left, remove the first stake, and put up his own, then the first one to reach the courthouse would receive the title. Later, the man quickest on the draw survived.

Many lives were lost in this way. The claim jumper was most unpopular, and if he was known as such he was not seen around camp for any length of time.

A group of men were discussing the latest victim of claim jumping. One man asked if anyone knew who shot him; no one answered directly, but one man said. "Well, you know Jim was the quickest man on the draw around camp." There were very few, if any, prosecutions. Claim jumping was held in the same category as horse stealing—men took the law into their own hands.

As the business grew, so did my parents' ambitions, and Mother wanted a house, and more room. It is surprising, in a rough mining camp, the fine people you meet, and the social gatherings. Card clubs and card parties were numerous, and required more room to entertain in the homes. Victor later had three churches, and many fraternal organizations were represented. It was before the day of motion pictures, although we now boasted an opera house. Being off the regular circuit, we had very few good shows, so the people enjoyed meeting in each other's homes. The popular game was high-five. Of course, for the men, especially the unmarried, there was no lack of entertainment; every gambling game generally found in camps —roulette wheels, fan bank, and ever the game of poker—found constant players in the saloons, sporting houses, and dance halls twenty-four hours of every day.

The Woods Investment Company had made a very rich strike in the Gold Coin Mine, located between our house and our store. The company consisted of the father, Mr. Woods, and two sons; and they were all very religious. They built a very elaborate shafthouse and office in which they held prayer meetings, until the little church they were constructing on Gold Coin property could be finished. They were of the Baptist faith, but the church they built seemed to be more or less a community affair. The first pastor of the church was a Dr. Ryder of Boston,

who came at the instigation of the Woods family. The state of
Mrs. Ryder's health may have had some bearing on his decision
to come to a mountain community. They had four little girls
and they had a struggle eking out a living on the meager salary
a preacher received at that time. Shortly thereafter the mother
died, leaving Dr. Ryder to get along as best he could.

The church became the center of social activities for young
and old. After the mine began producing in great quantities,
the continual raising and emptying of the ore buckets made so
much noise we were unable to hear the preacher, or anything
else that was said. The Woods family, being present at these
gatherings, decided that the church would have to be moved
to a less noisy location, and offered the use of some lots they
owned several blocks aways. The lots were adjacent to the sidewalk, but dropped abruptly some thirty or forty feet down a
gully; therefore almost the entire building had to be supported
on stilts, making it decidedly unsafe for occupancy, and it was
soon condemned.

We had a lawyer who served as organist. He had at one
time been a prominent attorney, but had lost his practice and
his health due excessive drinking. He came to my father and
told him he was not well and did not expect to live very long,
and requested that he not be buried in one of the backless
shrouds that were customary at that time, as he did not wish
to have to stand with his back against a telegraph pole on
resurrection day. Not long afterward we did bury him, and
in a shroud as his wife and family decided.

The new five-room house was built in a hurry. It looked
like a solid log house, but really the logs were split in half. The
chinking was white. There were two large pines in front and
several in the rear. Of course it was built on a hill, as there
was nothing but hills on which to build. The cost could not
have been too much, as there was no plumbing of any kind. We
bought water by the bucket from a man who had a large galvanized tank on a wagon, drawn by two heavy, strong horses.
They needed to be husky to pull the load of water over those
mountain roads. The water came from a very good spring, and

was cold and tested for impurities of all kinds. The tank had a rubber hose attached at the back and looked like an old sprinkler tank. I do not remember any deaths from typhoid or other fevers. We had a cistern with a pump built at the back door. Somehow it very seldom had much water in it, and when it did the water was rusty and dark. Mother, like all other thrifty housekeepers, had many ways of economizing on water. The bath water used by all the children on Saturday night was put in the largest galvanized washtub, and we took turns according to ages. I was last, of course, and Saturday night was the night I dreaded. My wildest dream was of the day we would have a bathtub, and I could have clean water and all I wanted of it. And that wasn't all that tub of water was used for. After the bath the soiled clothes were put to soak in it, and it was used for the first suds, as my mother called it. We also used the dishwater more than once if it wasn't too greasy. Clean water with which to scald them was also kept for future use.

The house was really nice, and we were proud of it. While it was not the most expensive in town, it certainly was the most attractive. It had a porch all the way across the front, and a platform at the south end by the kitchen door, which covered the cistern. After Father installed a hand pump, Mother had soft water for washing and household use. While it was never very clear-looking, it was a saving, and much better than the spring water we bought by the bucket from the water man, who delivered it by the large bucketful every other day. He also built me and my little sister Neva a playhouse back of the house. It was built from timber of quaking aspen trees; it had a good roof, two little windows, and a door. It was almost eight by nine feet, and while there was no chinking between the little logs, it was proof against rain and quite cozy. I swept the dirt floor often; it was so hard it was almost like cement.

I got an orange crate and nailed it to the wall, and a large box for a table and some small ones for stools. Mother gave me a small rug and some old cloth for window curtains. I was fourteen years of age, but still played with an old doll I had loved for years.

Here Tabby, the cat I had brought from the Springs, and I spent most of the daytime. I had my dolls and doll buggy, also a box with an old coat in it for Tabby's bed, and she slept out there nights. All was well until late in April, the next year, when we had one of those sudden terrific blizzards. If you have never lived in the mountains, you cannot realize how severe such blizzards can be. It luckily happened early one Saturday morning, and there was no school; otherwise there would have been no kittens and no story about them.

The first thought that I had was of Tabby and her four-day-old kittens; I knew the snow was blowing through those wide cracks. I couldn't stop for breakfast but bundled up and went to the rescue. Tabby was sitting up on the box cupboard. She was covered with ice and snow, and the box in which she had the kittens was full of snow. I dumped out the snow and four little hunks of ice.

Apparently the kittens were frozen stiff. Their little pink paws stuck out straight and were transparent, as were their tiny ears. I gathered them up and went weeping to the back door. Mother said not to bring them in as they were quite dead, but I guess she felt sorry for my grief and finally spread an old coat by the door on which to lay them while I went back for Tabby. She was so cold she could not walk so I carried her in and put her on a chair by the stove. She was so nearly frozen she didn't pay any attention to the kittens, but started immediately to wash herself and get warm. At that time everyone had coal stoves, so while my mother did not approve and objected strenuously to kittens in her oven, I argued they couldn't hurt if they were on an old coat. Then Spot, our beloved little dog, and I got busy and rolled and rubbed those little hunks of ice. He licked them with his big rough tongue, and whined, and I wept until Mother was quite upset. We gave Tabby some warm milk as soon as she thawed out a bit. She was busy with herself and paid no attention to us, and I doubt that she knew the kittens were there. It was fully an hour before any of them showed any sign of life, and then three of them began to open their mouths just a little and try to cry. Spot and I were delighted. By noon we had a cozy warm box with three little kittens in it, fully recovered and being fed and licked some more by their mother. I was happy, and stood by the box watching them, and Spot was curious and came and peeped over the edge of the box. And that ungrateful cat reached up and scratched him on his nose. They say cats have nine lives. I am sure they have at least two.

In a litter there is always one runt or weak one, and the tiny one did not survive. So later Spot and I held a funeral in the back yard.

My youngest brother, Burt, had several rabbit hutches out back; and one of the kittens, when it was old enough to run about and play, got on the wire top of a hutch where a doe had had her young rabbits, and fell in. The doe made short work of the kitten.

Another one met a sad fate. Aunt Amelia came up from Colorado City to stay with me and the two younger boys, while Father and Mother were on a buying trip to Kansas City, and to work days in the store. She came home to lunch, then left in a hurry and swung the screen door back. The door had a heavy spring. It shut with a bang and struck the little kitten. Aunt Amelia hurried right on down the street, and I gathered up the kitten. It was badly hurt, and since I had to hurry back to school, I put it under a box. When I came home it was dead. Only one kitten survived; it grew up to be a beautiful white tomcat. But since Tabby was very prolific, I had to give him away before the next litter arrived. They came at regular intervals. The very next time Tabby had kittens Aunt Amelia was visiting us, and to get even the kittens were born in her suitcase. Did I care?

One very cold night a woman called from the little town of Goldfield, about three miles from Victor, and said her husband had died and would the undertaker come right away. Father and one of the men were soon on their way in the Black Maria. The woman met them at the door and asked if they would mind stepping inside and waiting a few minutes as her husband was not yet quite dead. This certainly was most unusual and embarrassing; they said they would leave and come later when she should call them. She said she did not have a phone, and had walked several blocks to the house of a friend, who was one of the few to have one. While they were standing at the door discussing the situation, the man obligingly died and solved the problem.

In August, 1895, there was a lot of talk about a bullfight at Gillett. Grandmother Hunt, Aunt Amelia, and Uncle Billy had moved to Gillett and opened a new-and-used-furniture store there; and Uncle Billy often drove to Victor for supplies from our store. He told all about the bullfight—how they had so many carpenters and other laborers enlarging and remodeling the grandstand at the ball park, and how a matador and his wife, who was supposed to be the only lady bullfighter in the world, were coming from Chihuahua, Mexico, and bringing ten Mexican bulls they were going to kill at the fight. Father was excited, and immediately told my uncle to procure tickets for Sunday, as he intended to go. Mother said she thought it was cruel, and she was not going. She added that none of the children was going either. Father said he had no intention of taking her or anyone else.

Of course, we all wanted to go, but Father left by himself on Sunday morning. The first fight had been held on Saturday, August 24, in spite of the opposition of Colorado Springs church and humane societies. A large, excited crowd of three thousand witnessed the killing of the first bull. The bull put up a good fight, although he was not a Mexican bull. The United States Government had forbidden the entrance at the border of the ten bulls that were supposed to be entered for the fight, so they had to be replaced by local animals from the surrounding ranches. They had been able to buy a few. Before the applause of the excited crowd had subsided, the matador and his wife and other members of the troupe were arrested and taken to Gillett, and fined. But they were not held, and returned to continue the fight and dispatch two more bulls. It was, however, a complete fizzle, with an audience of only two or three hundred compared to the expected three thousand. Father said they had only five bulls, and they were just gentle, home-raised animals that refused to fight. So ended the first and only bullfight ever held in the district, or perhaps in the United States, for that matter.

Wherever there is progress you will find railroads. At first there was just the tiny narrow-gauge, the Florence and Cripple Creek, that wound around the mountains from Canyon City to Cripple Creek. This was the only means of transporting the ore from the mines to the smelter in Florence. As the mines began producing more heavily, this method was not satisfactory to the mine owners, as the ore taken from the mines had to be loaded into heavy wagons and hauled to the railroad, where it was dumped into open ore cars. Therefore the owners of the big producing mines decided to finance an extension of the Colorado Midland Railroad, which at that time passed through Divide, twenty miles distant, making direct contact with the mines in the district. Spurs were run below the mine dumps, where the ore was loaded from chutes directly into the ore cars, thus saving time and labor. From there it went directly to the mill, which had recently been constructed in Colorado City.

They decided to build a switch from the main line into Victor. In order to do so, they had to make two big cuts through the mountain. The formation was granite, and it was necessary to do a great deal of blasting with dynamite. At such times the people living in the immediate vicinity were warned to vacate their homes and go at least two blocks distant. Most of the houses were shacks, but our house was of sturdier construction, with a more sloping roof. And while some big rocks did occasionally fall on it, it was not damaged. Some of the smaller and more fragile houses were completely demolished, and the railroad assumed the responsibility for the damage.

One man batched in such a house, and his business was a cigar and magazine store, where men played solo in the rear room until all hours of the morning. He was in the habit of sleeping late, and since he did not open his place of business until noon, he did not heed their first warning. The second one was more insistent, as the blasting was very close to his house.

He rose reluctantly, pulled on his shoes and trousers, and went down the hill. Minutes later, when he returned, he found two tons of rock in the bed where he had been sleeping.

When the switch was completed, I had the distinction of riding the first train out of Victor. I was very ill with an attack of what was known as mountain fever, and the doctor, having done all he could for me, recommended that I be taken to a lower altitude. The train pulled down the track to the newly built depot at the north end of Fourth Street, about two blocks from our house. Through the courtesy of the railroad officials, arrangements had been made to stop the train out in front of our house and picked me up. I was placed on a cot and carried the short distance to the baggage car, where Mother rode beside me to Colorado City. There, I recuperated very rapidly, and in time to go back to school in the fall.

Mountain fever, like typhoid, causes the hair to fall out. Mine was true to form, and it came out until I had bald spots. I had always wanted curly hair, and had heard that if the hair was cut after a fever it would often come in curly. I couldn't have mine cut, and I always blamed the popular song "Chippy, Get Your Hair Cut" for Father's objection, because he said, "You know who you will look like, don't you?" It finally did grow again, but never very good and decidedly straight.

Nearly sixty years later, when the railroad into this district was discontinued, the event was commemorated by the presence of many prominent officials and citizens, the most distinguished being Lowell Thomas, who will long remember riding the last train out of Victor, while I will never forget riding the the first train out, though my ride was without pomp and ceremony. Lowell Thomas, with former Governor Carr, who was also a pioneer newspaper man of the district, and editor of the Victor *Record* at the time Lowell worked there, rode the last train on the old Midland Terminal out of Victor. Quite a difference between the two events! Both Victor and Cripple Creek had welcomed and honored the visitors. Merrill Shoup, president of the Golden Cycle Mill, was host to the fifty passengers who had traveled in the two cars from Colorado Springs.

The observation-lounge car, placed in service in 1887, and the old engine, Old 59—both, like the old towns in the district, were falling apart—were headed for the junk pile; but I have always had hopes that the district would boom again. All the great deposits of gold ore have not been discovered or mined. Just recently a very rich strike has been made in the Vindicator mine, one of the big producers that was handicapped by the heavy flow of water in the lower levels. The Carlton tunnel is draining these mines today and making it possible to operate and explore the levels hitherto inaccessible.

While the towns in the district have almost reached the ghost-town stage, there still is life and hope. Thousands of claims were staked during the rush, and the assessment work done, but they were not developed for lack of funds to continue. That doesn't prove they are worthless. There are thousands of acres still to be explored.

If ghosts walk the hillsides at night, they are legion and have no need to be lonely, if all the departed return.

There are a very few old-timers who have remained in the camp and lived in the same house fifty-three years. Among these are the A. W. Olivers, who are most worthy of mention. Mrs. Oliver assumed the charity work always in demand in any locality. She gave twenty-five years of service to the Red Cross and twenty-three years to public-welfare service, and only recently was forced to retire because of illness. I read two letters she received that bear testimony to the high esteem in which she is held. With her permission, I quote parts of the letters she received from the organizations. One from Governor Ed. C. Johnson, dated July 26, 1955, reads: "I am more than sorry that you are resigning as Director of Teller County's Public Welfare Dep't. I know that they shall miss you greatly. I am still very proud of the appointment I made back there in '35 and your wonderful record justifies every confidence placed in you by myself and all of your many friends." Guy R. Justis, director of the Department of Public Welfare, wrote: "Let me say personally how much I appreciate what you have done. I think only those who have been with the program since it started and have gone

through all the trials and tribulations, realize how much you
have given." Mr. John A. Dunn, personnel officer of the Department of Public Welfare, wrote: "I know it must be hard for you
after twenty-three years to leave the job which you have done
in a way that no one else could ever hope to equal, but you must
have ever so much satisfaction in knowing and remembering all
the people you have helped and the thousands of friends you
have made during your years of outstanding service." Mr. A. W.
Oliver was in the sampler business and bought gold from the
mines. They had one daughter, who married the principal of
the high school in Victor, Mr. William S. Roe, at the close of
his first year. Lowell Thomas was one of those graduated.
Later, Mr. Roe was principal of the Colorado Springs high
school for many years until his death. During his boyhood in
Victor, Lowell Thomas spent a great deal of his time with the
Olivers.

Victor claims a number of outstanding people who grew up
in mining camps and later left and made names for themselves, but by far the most noted is Lowell Thomas, known all
over the world as a celebrated and beloved commentator and
announcer. Whenever his name is mentioned, I hasten to claim
him, and always add, "Oh, yes, he was a Victor boy." Lowell
came to Victor when he was three years old, with his parents.
His father, Dr. Harry G. Thomas, practiced medicine there when
the district was a booming camp of seventy thousand people.
Lowell was graduated from Victor High School in 1909—it was
the thirteenth graduating class and there were thirteen grad-
uates, which should entirely eliminate, as far as he is concerned,
any superstition about unlucky thirteen. He was an outstanding
pupil of unusual oratorical ability, beloved by teachers and
fellow students. He was editor of his school paper *The Sylvanite*, a career he later followed a short time as editor of the
Victor *Record*, getting his start with the paper as delivery boy
during his grade-school days. Later, he also worked on the
Cripple Creek *Times*. He left the district to attend institutions
of higher learning, and, as all know, his career has taken him
far up the heights in the realms of travel, journalism, and radio.

Since the family business had outgrown the building it occupied, a new building was planned and built on the corner of Fourth and Diamond streets. There were really two large store rooms with connecting doors, one for the furniture and one for undertaking. The upstairs was quite a large rooming house. There must have been thirty rooms, and we also had a deck, and it was a real one. It extended out about a fourth of the way one one side and across the back end of the furniture store. By now we carried a much better grade of new furniture, with less secondhand furniture and a really fine line of china and glassware, and on the deck, up a not-too-good open stairway, was proudly displayed our very finest furniture and dishes.

It was my job to dust it, and in my spare time I was the clerk. Many beautiful sets of Haviland china were sold from that deck. People had money, and spent it. I have the set my father gave to Mother, also a set an aunt bought, to which I fell heir. It will be handed down to the next generation.

One day a lady wearing a flowing cape came into the store. She browsed for some time in the china department, but did not make a purchase. After she left, Father noticed a Haviland cup was missing from its saucer. A few days later she returned. Father picked up the saucer, which was still on the counter, and as he handed it to her he said, "Here is the saucer to your cup. Now don't ever come in here again."

When the first building on North Fourth Street was completed, the undertaking department was greatly improved. It consisted of three rooms. The one in the rear was called the morgue. Here the body was prepared for burial; it was laid out on the cooling board, and in most cases embalmed. If it was a woman or a child, I helped with the dressing and combed the hair.

The other rear room was for caskets. We had improved on the stock of what at first had been the original shape of wooden coffins, now these were more of a box shape and cloth-covered. Some were covered with a brocaded velveteen in pale shades; some were white; others a pale pink, called ashes of roses; and there were also a few metallic caskets for special, high-priced burials. A two-hundred-dollar funeral was a top price, and they were rare.

The front room, with a street entrance, was the largest room. There was a carpet on the floor, and chairs to seat a large number of mourners and friends. Here the funeral services were held.

We had competition in the undertaking business. Up to this time we had been the only ones in the business in Victor; and Hallett and Baker, the only firm in Cripple Creek. A Mr. Dunn had established his business on South Fourth Street in Victor, and Lampman Undertaking Company now had a place on West Bennet Avenue in Cripple Creek. Both new firms were Catholic. Before this there had been no question of religion; if we had the choice of a minister, Father would call a pastor of one of the several denominations now in Victor. Sometimes the pastor would inquire about the financial standing of those concerned, and if unfavorable he would be too busy to officiate. Father Downey, a broad-minded, kindly priest, was never too busy, nor was he interested in pay for his services. Often he and my father made the final trip with the Black Maria, and, with the sexton, were the only ones present at the burial. On the very rare occasions when Father Downey was unable to attend, Father drove to the cemetery alone. He had bought a small book and would read a short burial service out of it, with the ever-present sexton as the only listener.

And now a most disgraceful procedure came into the picture. Since Charles Hallett was coroner, in cases of accidental death it was the law that the body was not to be touched or moved until he had arrived and investigated the cause of death. It depended upon the location of the scene; if it was closer to Victor, we were notified; and if the distance to Cripple Creek was shorter, someone came from Hallett's place of business to remove the body or bodies. But now it was different. While he could designate the place the inquest was to be held, it didn't mean that was where the funeral was to be held. As soon as the news of a suicide or violent death got around, and it got around fast, the two interested factions got busy and found out the religion, fraternal organizations, business associates, family, and friends, if the deceased had any; and they were contacted immediately. If the deceased's family had called the undertaker, in case of a death where no coroner was required, the bereaved family was contacted by the competitor and his friends, and every possible pressure brought to bear on why the body should be removed from one undertaker to the other one. It became a disreputable racket, a tug-of-war, one to hold the case, as it was called, and the other pulled every string in his power to take it away. It was a situation we at least disliked heartily, but not to the extent that we didn't do our share of "stiff snatching." When the competitor went to claim the body, he was accompanied by one or more of his backers, who would have a written order. There was no violence, just a battle of words. As soon as possible the body was embalmed, and then if they were forced to allow the other undertaker to remove the corpse to his place of business, he could not do so until he paid the fifty-dollar fee charged for such services. Sometimes they proved to be paupers, and the county allowed only thirteen dollars for burial; then the undertaker was out his time and embalming fluid. Such instances did not often occur, and never when the deceased was a woman. If she happened to be a girl from the red-light district, and she had been shot or had committed suicide, the madam and the other girls took up a collection and gave her a decent burial. Such girls were most careful to have no means of identification, as they did not want their relatives to know the kind of life they were living.

While there were heated arguments at such times, and verbal insults exchanged, such as "chaws" and "red necks" and unprintable names, there never was any violence in Victor; but Charlie Hallett met up with more than an argument in Cripple Creek. Once he arrived to remove a body and suffered a severe beating, only to find the corpse in question had already been rushed to Mount Pisgah Cemetery and had been buried that same day. Mother especially disapproved of such practices, and said that to take advantage of a bereaved family at such times was unkind, to say the least. Once Mother met Mr. Dunn, our competitor, at a social gathering, and she said he was a real nice gentleman—not the monster he had been painted to be.

Of course, we lost some business, but the camp was growing, and there were more deaths, and we still had our share, especially of accidental deaths. We buried all the victims of the three major disasters: the cave-in at the Annie Lee Mine, the cage at the Stratton Independence, and the dynamiting of the platform at Independence at the depot.

This was really the heyday of the Cripple Creek district. We, with others, were really making money. The store was stocked with good merchandise; but, sorry to say, the undertaking department was the busiest and most remunerative. Both my brothers passed the State Board and became licensed embalmers; so they, with what Father called his pensioners, old friends who had followed us, and a doctor who had had an unfortunate family affair and just drifted in, constituted the working staff, and all were kept busy.

CHAPTER VIII

CHARACTERS

Throughout the years we had many interesting characters working for us; they slept at the store but they boarded with us.

First, there was Jack Peacock, whom we had known in Wisconsin and Kansas. He was the little hunchback who, when he first came to Colorado City, prospected with Shorty George. He was about four feet four, and Shorty George was six feet six. People called them Mutt and Jeff. Before Jack Peacock worked for us, they had batched in a little shack not far from our place, and my brother Gil and I often went there to have supper with them. Peacock would sit by the stove in our kitchen and "smuk" his old pipe and, much to Mother's disgust, push back any skillet or kettle she might have on the stove, lift the stove lid, and spit in the fire. She stood for it for a while, but finally got him "told off." He pretended to think a lot of Barney, our beloved horse, but we all knew he was mean to him. At times he would jerk him cruelly. The horse had a very tender mouth, and we would see blood oozing at the corners, caused by the bit. We accused him of it, but he would just go on telling us that Barney was a grand horse. And believe it or not, both he and my father would shed tears. Mother said "crocodile tears." He had a wife, son, and daughter in Kansas who refused to live with him because he was so cruel to the stock. He was an old man, and soon left us to spend his remaining days with relatives in California.

One day Shorty George told us about the time when he was ten years old. He lived on a farm somewhere in the east. His father gave him a nickel and sent him to a store three miles distant to buy a bag of tobacco. When he arrived at the store he was unable to find the money. He searched every pocket to no avail—the money was lost; but the kindly storekeeper let him have the tobacco anyway, and he hurried home, knowing full well what awaited him when his father found out about the loss of the money. And he had reason to worry, for his father gave him the worst beating he had ever had. It was also the last. That evening he sat down by the wood box in the kitchen to whittle awhile before going to bed. When he took out his pocket knife, there was the nickel, caught in a groove where there was a broken knife blade. He showed it to his mother, then went to his room, picked up a few belongings, left home, and somehow managed to make his living. He never returned nor did he ever see his parents or family again, although in later years he did write to his mother to tell her he was alive and well.

Then there was Judge McCoach, an attorney we had known in Kansas. His wife had died in childbirth, as also had the little son. He never got over it; he was very bitter. He went to Alaska soon after. Somehow both his feet were so badly frozen that part of them were amputated nearly to the ankle. He had to wear special custom-made shoes. He was a prominent Mason, and organized several of the Masonic lodges in Colorado. He claimed to be an infidel and read all Bob Ingersoll's books. He was Patron when I was initiated in Victoria Chapter, O.E.S., and at the banquet that preceded the initiations he presided and asked the blessing. I asked him about it afterward and he gave me a very evasive answer. Years later, when he was a very old man, he came back to Colorado City, and his aged sister came and kept house for him. He eventually became a Christian Scientist and a very devout Christian. He was a fine man, and I cannot believe he was really ever an infidel.

Doc Benedict, the last man who worked for us and boarded at our home, was really a character. He was the last but by no means the least of our help. He came to the store one day and asked for a job. He was a very neatly dressed man in his early forties; in fact, he was so well dressed that my father hesitated to tell him what kind of work he would have to do. His clothes were expensive and certainly tailor-made; and he was an educated, refined gentleman. He was also very quiet and brokenhearted. Much later he told my father he was a doctor and had had a good practice in a small town in the East. He had also owned and operated the only drugstore in the town. He was doing fine, he said, until he had domestic trouble. Apparently he adored his wife. But whatever was the trouble, he gave her everything they owned—the drugstore, the home—and since then he had never practiced medicine again. He had presented her with his doctor's bag, and left. That was the only time he mentioned his past life.

Being a doctor, he fitted beautifully into the undertaking department; he was willing, capable, and always the perfect gentleman. Since someone had to be at the undertaking parlor day and night, he occupied the room in the rear of the store. His duties were many and varied; he kept the furniture and crockery department neat and clean, took care of the large heating stove, carried coal and ashes, helped sew long seams of carpet, made deliveries, and occasionally directed a funeral. He was very easy to please, and always thanked Mother for any special dish she served. He carried his dishes to the kitchen after he had eaten. About once in a month or six weeks, he wouldn't show up for breakfast. We children did not know why, but our parents knew; he would go on a periodical drunk for two or three days. Mother had a quart milk can with a lid, and she would send it to him full of coffee. When he finally showed up for a meal, he would look ashamed. We were told not to mention his absence when Doc was under the weather.

One day we had a funeral in Cripple Creek and Doc drove the hearse from Victor. He was late getting back. Finally a phone call came from Anaconda, a little town between Cripple Creek and Victor, saying that a man who was driving our hearse had fallen off the seat, and was lying unconscious on the sidewalk, where he had been laid. One of the boys got a saddle horse and went over to bring him and the hearse back, and since he couldn't sit up, the most logical thing to do was put him inside the hearse. There was a special stall at the livery barn where we kept the hearse, the Black Maria, and the horses, so my brother backed the hearse in its regular stall, opened the door a crack, and left him there to wake up. Doc had a key to the rear door of the store, so no one ever saw him crawl out of that hearse (or in the street, or at the store). What do you think his reaction was when he wakened and realized he was in the hearse? No one ever mentioned it, and you may be sure he did not. When it was mentioned at home with a laugh, we were told Doc had a sunstroke; and that is what they said at Anaconda, when they went for him. I wonder how many believed it!

Once when my little brother Burt was sick, Mother asked Doc to look at him to see whether he had measles or scarlet fever. Doc told her he wasn't practicing medicine, but finally he did look him over and said it could be either. Burt said he had had every kind of measles, a different kind every spring when he was little, and he was sure it must be scarlet fever, as he peeled afterward.

Doc was with us four or five years, and then left just as abruptly as he had come. A few weeks later we heard he was in St. Francis Hospital in Colorado Springs. I happened to be staying with my married sister Myrtie, helping with the children, that summer, so I went to see him. He was in the charity ward, and I would never have recognized him if he hadn't spoken to me. Normally he was a small man (he always wore a mustache); now he was a fat man, terribly bloated, and with mustache and beard. He was very, very sick and seemed embarrassed to have me see him. He mentioned he needed a shave. My father went to see him. He said he knew he was sick when he left Victor, but didn't want anyone to know. He didn't want to be a burden. I saw him just the one time, as he only lived a few days afterward. My father was the only one to attend his funeral. Father also paid for it. He died alone and unloved. Such a wasted life, for one who could really have been someone! During his stay with us, to our knowledge, he never received or wrote a letter, and left nothing that would help in notifying his people.

One day Father had business in Cripple Creek, and saw a man he had known in Colorado City. He was a very tall man, at least six feet six inches, who was in the habit of occasionally overindulging in the cup that cheers. At such times he was very sociable. He was entertaining a group of men in front of the saloon on Bennett Avenue. He climbed up to sit on a large empty beer barrel, the top of which was loosely fitted. It immediately caved in, jackknifing him tightly into the barrel, with only his arms and legs protruding. He was so tightly wedged that the men couldn't extricate him until they turned the barrel on its side and rolled it. It required five men to get him out, one for each arm and leg and one to roll the barrel. He was a good sport about it though, and joined in the hilarious laughter of the crowd that had gathered around.

CHAPTER IX

FIRES

The first big fire in Cripple Creek occurred on April 26, 1896. It was started by the overturning of a gasoline stove during a scuffle. All the buildings were wooden structures, and most of the time at that altitude it is quite dry, and the buildings were like so much kindling. The southeastern section, where the sporting houses, cribs, dance halls, and saloons were located, was the first to catch fire. It burned so rapidly that the inmates barely had time to reach safety. A few were not so fortunate, and died; others were badly burned.

Victor responded to the call for help as quickly as possible, but the heavy horse-drawn equipment, including our new chemical truck, was nearly an hour in reaching the scene. Since there was a high wind, the fire had spread to other sections of the town, and they were of little assistance. The Cripple Creek equipment and some of Victor's were entirely useless, as the small reservoir was nearly empty and there was absolutely no pressure. Buildings were dynamited in an effort to stop the spread of the flames, but the blast and the wind scattered the boards, and they added fuel to the fire.

This fire destroyed the southeastern and eastern sections of Cripple Creek, including Bennett Avenue. It lasted three hours, and very little of the property was covered by insurance.

At quarter of two in the afternoon the following Wednesday, another fire broke out on the corner of Myers and Second streets. It started in the Portland Hotel when a kettle of grease was overturned and caught fire. As usual it was a very windy day. The fire lasted until late evening, and the buildings that had escaped the Saturday fire went up in smoke. Many were homeless, and Colorado Springs came to the rescue. A special train brought food, bedding, and tents.

While the fire ruined many businessmen, they were a brave

lot, and soon Cripple Creek was being rebuilt, this time mostly of brick construction.

It took more than fire to dampen the spirit of those enterprising businessmen of Victor and Cripple Creek. But the financial loss was too heavy for some, and they were unable to recover their former prosperity. There were many business failures.

Our furniture store in Victor did a tremendous business, and my father had become a wealthy merchant. There was no mortgage on the building, stock, two hearses, or any of the equipment. He owned a large block of Ajax mine stock. And the outstanding bills alone would have been a small fortune at that time, a large percentage of which were never paid. One thing he did not have was insurance; and while Victor now had a small reservoir, the pressure was never good at any time.

On Christmas Day, 1898, David Heaton and I were married and left on a honeymoon to visit his brother and his family in Utah. My brother-in-law was a conductor on the Colorado Midland. (His run was between Colorado City and Leadville.) So there would be no doubt about our being newlyweds, he passed the information on to the crew who took over at Leadville. They played all kinds of practical jokes on us, the last one being in Grand Junction. The Wells Fargo agent at this station had recently been transferred from Victor, and he and his family were personal friends of ours, so my husband inquired of the conductor how long a stop we would have there. He said twenty minutes. The office was upstairs, and he had barely reached it when he looked out the window and saw the train moving. He ran down the stairs and down the track. The train kept right on moving, the conductor, brakeman, and porter waving good-by to him from the back platform. I was unaware of all this until the porter came in and said, "Is you got a man?"

Of course, I thought I had. He told me then that he had been left at Grand Junction. The conductor came back and said not to worry; I could go on to my destination; and he invited me to be his dinner guest. However, soon a telegram from the bridegroom came, telling me to get off at a small station and wait for him; which I did. There was no time to prepare for my hurried exit from that train. I had on a pair of fancy white bedroom slippers topped with white fur. There was no time to change them. With my baggage I was hustled to the back platform and dropped off at a tiny depot, the only building at the station.

It was very cold and there were several inches of snow on the ground. There I stood, right in the middle of nowhere in my fancy white fur-topped slippers and my coat, my hat, with its big feather on one side, suitcases, and a broken box of toys we were taking to the children, out of which fell tiddly-de-winks and small toys. I was annoyed and bewildered, and did not return the trainmen's waves as the train pulled out and left me standing there.

The station agent just stared and laughed, and I laughed with him. He helped me carry my things into the depot, and I explained my sudden appearance to him and his wife, when she emerged from the living quarters they occupied in the rear of the depot. Then all three of us laughed, and I think I was a bit hysterical. I didn't know at the time about the trainmen's joke and blamed my bridegroom for the predicament in which I found myself. We were thirty miles from Grand Junction, and it took several hours to drive a horse and buggy that distance; but I was made quite welcome and was invited to dinner. The time passed more quickly than it would have had I just sat in the depot. It was late that night when we returned to Grand Junction, and spent a couple of very pleasant days with our friends, the Brookses.

When we returned to Victor, after the honeymoon, we discovered our friends had sent a notice to the Victor *Record* about our unexpected visit and full details of what led up to it. Since we were well known, there was plenty of razzing.

Shortly after we returned from our honeymoon, we moved to a little town northeast of Victor, about three miles distant, and with our friend Dr. Ryder, the minister at the little church who had married us, bought a prosperous little grocery store, owned and operated by the Henley brothers. None of us knew anything about the grocery business. While I had clerked in my father's furniture and crockery store, this was entirely different. Dr. Ryder had no business experience, and my husband was interested only a very short while; then he spent most of his time looking for mining property he could lease.

Since the miners were paid the first of each month, most of our business was on credit. I kept the books and helped in the store when needed. We had two clerks and a driver to take orders and deliver groceries.

To prove how inexperienced we were, one day I was helping Dr. Ryder check an invoice, and he said, "One five-pound box of doctor apples" (dr. apples—dried), and later one case of George Washington beans (golden wax—G.W.). At the end of six months we turned the store back to the Henley brothers, and that was the end of our business venture. Later we sold our little three-room house and moved to one about a mile and half from Victor, to a little new addition called Hollywood.

The following March, my older sister Myrtie died. Of course all of us were deeply grieved, especially since there were two very small girls to be taken care of, who would miss her loving care. My father was heartbroken, as she had worked with him and was very close, and since he had worked very hard and needed a vacation and rest, and my husband and I were capable and willing to look after the business, Father and Mother, with little sister Neva, decided to take a trip to California. They could well afford the hard-earned vacation.

Before they left, they had moved again, very much against Mother's wishes. Their new home was directly back of the new store, at the end of the lot. It was a two-story structure covered with a metal imitation of brick. It was not as attractive as our log house; and none of us liked it except Father. He said it was so much handier to the store, and we did have water in the house sometimes, and a bathroom.

The town had had some controversy over the new water supply. Water was finally piped into the district, but at times there was no pressure. Only a few houses had bathrooms because of this uncertainty. Of course this situation was the reason for the prohibitive fire-insurance rates. The businessmen called a meeting, and all agreed not to carry insurance, but to improve the volunteer fire department and buy a new chemical fire engine.

One windy day, just a few weeks after the folks had left, a girl who wore one of those bright-red wrappers and whose hair was cut very short, and curled, and who occupied one of the little shacks that constituted what they called "The Row," decided to clean one of her dresses with gasoline. She did clean it—and she cleaned the whole town. Every business building burned to the ground, and a few homes that stood nearby, like ours, were destroyed.

I lived only about three miles distant. After the alarm was spread, I ran all the way over the mountainside to Victor. The fire was already crossing the tracks about half a block from the store and our house. It is surprising how things disappear at such exciting times. The house seemed full of people, and it was hard to know whether they were helping to save things or helping themselves. Drawers that were packed with Mother's hand-drawn and embroidered linens were taken out of the chests and disappeared. Someone did help pack and carry the Haviland china to a safe place, and also a few prized family pictures.

One woman had just started dinner. The boiled potatoes were half done, and she picked up the kettle and ran with it. When she realized what she had done, she was on the hillside with nothing but the hot kettle. Nothing else mattered; she had saved the potatoes.

The men at the livery barn saved all the horses, including our beloved Barney and a white horse called Bodey we had bought to drive with him on the white hearse, but both hearses and the wagon we called the Black Maria, a light wagon covered with black oilcloth that was used to bring the corpse to the undertaking room, were burned, as were all the equipment and the furniture in the store and undertaking parlor.

We had a trained magpie, a shiny black-and-white bird, in a large cage fastened to the coal shed at the rear. I tried to get him, but he was so frightened he flew back into the farthest corner, and I could not reach him. The last thing I heard as I hurried away from the burning building was Maggie frantically calling my brother's name. Poor Maggie! Poor also all the good folks who had struggled and worked, and just as their dreams seemed realized, awoke to a nightmare.

We dreaded sending the telegram that put an abrupt end to the vacation, but we knew Mother and Father would hear about it through the newspapers at once. There was no use trying to cover up. All it could say was: "Victor burned to the ground."

By the time they got home, the boys had set up a large tent where the store had stood. They got undertaking supplies from the main branch in Cripple Creek, and were carrying on the business. Many others did the same, and Victor became a tent city.

They say you cannot keep a good man down, and those brave and dauntless men who had lost their all did not stand around and bemoan their losses. They pitched right in and said they would build a bigger and better Victor; and the new town grew, and it was better. Most of it was made of brick. Labor was scarce, and the businessmen who had made their fortunes, and had had others do most of their work for them before the fire, could be seen in overalls working as they had when they first came to the camp as poor men, and had built their own frame buildings, as there was no one to do the hard work for them. They mortgaged everything they possessed to get money for the new buildings.

My father had quite a sum on deposit, but nowhere near enough to build and buy new stock for the store and the undertaking parlor. He had sold or traded to the Ajax Mining Company his interest in a mine located just north of where I had found the pocket of shiny ore, taking stock in that mine instead of cash. It was quite valuable stock, as the mine was among the richest producers and still is. This stock was put up as collateral for the money borrowed at the bank. He also bought back the little log house where we all had been so proud and happy, and soon it was their home again.

CHAPTER X

STRIKES

In 1893 and 1894 the district had its second strike. This time it was a sympathetic strike. The Standard Mill at Colorado City was having union trouble, and the workers went out. They were hiring scab labor, and union miners were mining the ore that was shipped to the mill, so the miners refused to work.

The district had been almost unanimously in sympathy with the miners during the first strike. Their demands were fair—a three-dollar, eight-hour day—but they were disturbed by the violence and the loss of life, so they were reluctant to go through another such experience. However, there was nothing to be done about it.

If you have never lived in a community during a strike, you have no idea what it means. People who have been friends and neighbors for years become suspicious of each other, and bitter enemies. Little children who played together on the hillside and had loved each other fought and were unhappy and were afraid to go to the store on an errand because they might get into a street brawl. Women who had visited and gossiped together no longer spoke to each other unless it was in an insulting way. Men who had waited for each other to go to work together, carrying their dinner pails, now went their separate ways carrying concealed deadly weapons with which to destroy each other. Those who went to work were stoned by women and children along the way and called vile names—and all were called scabs.

It was extremely difficult for the businessmen; there was no way they could remain neutral. If a customer who had traded with a merchant for years was seen in his store by the opposition, the word got around and he was boycotted.

The union constructed a bull pen where anyone who scabbed, or was suspected of not being in sympathy with the strikers, was handled roughly and imprisoned.

Men who had lived peaceably with their next-door neighbors were spied upon, and the least suspicious move was reported. Friendships were forgotten. It was war, and each side meant to win. Men were tried and sent to prison for some of the crimes committed. Others went unpunished.

There was friendly rivalry between Victor and Cripple Creek. Cripple Creek had the name of being the district, but Victor had the mines. And it also had most of the tragedies.

In 1903, my husband decided to visit his family in England. He had not seen them since he had come to the United States eighteen years before. So with our little boy, Earl, who was now three years of age, we sailed in June and were gone three months. On our return we spent most of the time in the East, so what happened during our absence was written to us by my parents. They described in detail the horrors attending the blowing up of the Independence depot, the cage falling down the shaft at the Independence mine, how the dismembered victims were brought to the mortuary and laid out on long tables and covered with sheets, and the heartbreaking scenes of families and friends trying to reassemble the bodies of what had been their loved ones.

One woman came in and carefully put together what she was sure had been her husband, only to be followed a little later by another woman who identified the body as her husband, and proved it by old scars on the body. The two women insisted on their separate claims right up the funeral. Months later one quietly had her supposed husband disinterred and shipped to the Colorado Springs cemetery. If the other one ever found out about it, we did not know, but there was no further questioning.

When the cage at the Independence, which was a crude, double-decked, open elevator, brought up the day shift, the cable snapped, and it dropped to the bottom of the shaft. One man was able to jump off before it entered the shaft and was miraculously saved. The others were scattered in sections at each drift as the cage flew by. No one man was found intact at any level.

There was no way the bodies could be thoroughly embalmed,

but great quantities of formaldehyde were used to preserve them until relatives could make some kind of identification. After all were separated and reassembled, the remaining unidentified parts were buried in a common grave with all the names on the marker of the parts unclaimed by the others.

The levels the cage passed were underground tunnels dug at given depths to explore and remove the ore from the mine. They were built as safely as possible, being held by strong timbers to prevent the walls and ceilings from caving in. However, with all the care, many men lost their lives from cave-ins.

Mrs. Oliver referred me to Mr. Stern, who was indefinite about details, but said he thought there were thirteen men on the cage. I think there were eighteen.

It was nerve-racking and pitiful to see the grief of the bereaved, and the tension caused by the tragedy. Of course, some blamed the engineer, but it was later more or less proved that the cable or some part of the hoist had been tampered with. The union was blamed for this, but it was never definitely proved, or the blame established; but certainly whoever committed the atrocity must have felt he had done a most complete job.

There were plenty of shooting scrapes and several deaths, but the most shocking events were the two mentioned above. The Labor Day riot was quite exciting, but only one man was killed outright. Several, however, were wounded.

It was customary to hold celebrations on Labor Day. There would be all kinds of races and contests, the principal one being the drilling contest. A huge block of granite would be hauled in and placed on a rudely constructed platform, so that the crowd could watch and cheer or boo the contestants. The men who were considered the best drillers were chosen from the different mines. Two men made up the required drill team— one to wield the heavy hammer, the other to hold the steel bar and pour water in the hole. They used huge hammers, and the steel bars were driven into the granite just as it was done in the mines. Sticks of dynamite were dropped in the holes to blast the rock. But at the Labor Day exhibition the holes made were only measured to see who could drill the deepest in a given time, and no dynamite was used. The winner received a prize, generally in gold pieces.

These celebrations were held at different places, sometimes at a beautiful natural park called Pinnacle Park, about five miles north of Victor. Nearly always someone was killed or hurt in fights at these times. During the strike, the celebration was held on a vacant corner in the center of town, just across from the union hall, where the Victor Hotel had been before the fire. A union meeting was being held at the time the rioting started, and the front of the union hall still bears the marks of the bullets that struck it. The windows were shot out, the meeting was hurriedly broken up, and the men joined the rioters and added to the violence. Excitement ran high for many days. Arrests followed, but little could be done about it.

Sherman Bell, who was a captain in the state militia, had a room at Mother's over the undertaking parlor. He was present at the celebration, and when violence broke out he immediately took steps to quell the riot, but was unsuccessful, and only added to the confusion. The militia had been ordered out by Governor Waite, who represented a newly formed political party known as the Populist Party, which itself created a great deal of disturbance.

Eventually the strike was settled, but the camp began gradually going down, the way all camps do. One reason was that the mines by this time had become quite deep, and the cost and danger in keeping the water out was becoming too great. The water had to be pumped out. Also the cost of shipping ore to the mill at the Springs was quite high, although we now had a wide-gauge railroad, whereas in the earlier days much of the ore was hauled in large wagons pulled by four or six husky horses. And about this time a number of mines found the rich veins exhausted, and the ore was of lower grade. The ore was sorted and the high-grade ore dumped into wagons, while the lower grade was thrown on the dumps. Later, when the price of gold went from twenty dollars an ounce to thirty-five, many of these dumps were worked over at a profit. The mill dump in

Colorado City was later used for paving the streets of Colorado Springs, and it has been said that the streets in Colorado Springs were paved in gold.

So in spite of all anyone could do, the camp slipped lower and lower. Business fell off steadily, and one after the other the worthy businessmen were closed out and left with nothing. My parents were among them. The mining stock long ago had been taken over by the bank; the mortgage on the furniture was foreclosed; and finally the building itself was sold for taxes.

Years later, when I made a trip to the camp, there wasn't a brick left of that large two-story building. It had been about 150 long by 75 feet wide. The lumber and bricks must have been hauled out of the district, as no new homes or buildings were constructed. It was very depressing to me, yet it was marvelous how those men who had failed through no fault of their own went other places, and began again to build up businesses and homes, some even again to become quite prosperous. Of course, some were so crushed that they made little or no effort to do more than just live.

I know now how great the blow was to my father, although at the time he made a great effort to cover up his discouragement, and appeared quite enthusiastic about the next ventures ahead.

The first move was to Greeley, Colorado. They drove the same white horse, Barney, and while they liked the beautiful little city, the business was a failure.

The camp still had its lure, and back they went. There was a vacant two-story building in a central location in Victor, so they lived upstairs and rented the few extra rooms. Again the room downstairs was divided into two sections, one for caskets and a workroom, and the other for the chapel—and, of course, the deck. But it was not used for display this time, but for rough boxes and storage. It was exclusively an undertaking establishment.

CHAPTER XI

HELPERS IN TIME OF NEED

Flowers that bloom in high altitudes are especially beautiful, as the shades are so much deeper and the blooms larger. There was a hill back of the school, and I discovered that on the other side of it, in a little valley, the first anemones bloomed in a secluded spot the latter part of May. I was late getting home one night after school, as I had to pick those first lovely flowers. They were a deep lavender, cup-shaped, something like buttercups. The leaves were a silver green and they had a little ruff around them of soft feathery silver. Later, they would be found growing profusely on the hillsides, but the stems were not so long nor the colors so deep. The spot was fully a mile from school. I always went alone, so that no one else would know my secret. It was an isolated spot, and I never met anyone there, nor was I afraid. In spite of the wildness of the country and the many tragedies, I never heard of a girl or woman being molested in the district.

Considering the hardships women endured in a new western community without modern conveniences, there were no divorces, and women seldom became dissatisfied with conditions and left their homes and husbands to return to more modern cities or their former homes. There was a fascination about the life and always some excitement, and, of course, the hope of becoming rich. Men seemed to recognize the rights and sacredness of other men's homes; but if they were deceived, they took matters into their own hands.

One Labor Day when the district was having a big public picnic at Pinnacle Park, a beautiful natural park at the foot of Bull Hill, a young woman who was engaged to be married to a certain young man boarded the train in Independence, a small town between Victor and the park, with another man. Her fiancé, who had been informed of her intentions, was on the train, and promptly shot her. If there was a trial or conviction, I do not remember it.

When death or disaster overtook the needy or sick, help, strange to say, came from those who frequented the saloons and gambling houses, where a quick and generous response was always forthcoming.

Among the many who came to the gold camp to make their fortunes, and perhaps to leave behind some unpleasantness, was a very young man, nineteen or twenty years of age. He was a quiet, refined person. Education and personality were decidedly evident, and we felt sure he came from a good family. The name he gave us must have been fictitious, as we could never trace his identity. He did odd jobs for my father in the furniture store, and seemed to understand a great deal about the undertaking business. At night, like most men and grown boys, he would walk about town and drop in to watch the gambling games. He had no money and did not play in the games or drink. One night there was an argument over cards, and as was customary those concerned settled the argument in one way —the survivor was the one quickest on the draw. Being unused to such procedure, he stepped between the two men and, of course, was killed. We felt very sorry about it as we had grown to like the young man. We tried every way to locate his people; he had told us nothing about them, or about himself, and we never knew who his people were or where he had lived. I wonder if they grieved and hoped for his return in vain.

Community chests and such organizations as we have today were nonexistent; and while I do not wish to disparage the churches, which were very few for a long time, it was not the churches that helped the poor and unfortunate when disaster fell. It was the miners, the men who frequented the saloons and gambling tables, and the girls from the dance halls who laid their silver dollars on the line. And last but by no means least was that wonderful B.P.O.E. organization. No one will ever know all the charities and human kindnesses that it not only preached but practiced.

There was a little girl whose home and entire family were

buried by the dump slide of one of the large mines. She became their ward. They maintained her, and no little girl ever had more devoted parents.

It was the day before Christmas and like everyone else I was busy preparing for the big day. Our little boy, Earl, was nineteen months old, and it would be the first Christmas tree he would enjoy. We were decorating the tree when Father called and said that a woman had died, and as usual I must go with him. In a few minutes he came, and we took Earl to Mother's and then left in the Black Maria for Anaconda, a small settlement about four miles distant.

The Anaconda mine, now a heavy producer, had built a mill in the gulch below the mine, and there were a few small shacks near it to house the mill workers and their families. We stopped at one of these, and upon being admitted found the bewildered little family grouped around a small cook stove in the one room used as a kitchen, dining room, and living room.

There were five children. The eldest, a girl of about ten, was holding the youngest, a small child wrapped in a blanket. The father took us into the other room in which there were crowded three double beds. There was no evidence of the body until a feather bed was turned back. (It was the German custom to use a tick filled with feathers as a coverlet instead of a mattress, as I had always seen it used.) The tiny wasted form scarcely made a wrinkle. She had died of tuberculosis and had been ill for a long time.

On our return trip to the undertaking parlor, we were very quiet, and both of us were doing a lot of thinking about the sad scene we had just witnessed.

I finally said, "I know what I'm going to do."

Father said, "I think I know. And I have been thinking the same thing. I'm going to call the Exalted Ruler of the Elks and report this family, who are so in need of help."

The Benevolent Order of Elks was certainly well named. The Elks took over and a committee was dispatched as quickly as possible, with baskets of food, and to assist in preparing the house for Christmas Day. They ascertained the ages of the children and sent appropriate toys, some needed clothing, and a Christmas tree. I am sure that family never had partaken of a more bounteous, well-prepared Christmas dinner; and I doubt that any of them did afterward. The next day, when the father came to make the final funeral arrangements, he told us how grateful he was to those wonderful people for their help and kindness at his time of greatest need.

One day when a funeral was being conducted in the chapel, I heard singing—which was unusual. I peeked in the side door and saw our little mother standing up in front with a song book, singing without accompaniment, as we had no organ or piano. She was singing "Rock of Ages" in her sweet soprano voice. When she finished and sat down, I felt like applauding, which on such a solemn occasion would have been out of place. The district at this time did not boast of a soloist, or at least we did not know of one.

I never see those gaudy artificial wreaths and sprays on display in our stores today at a certain season without thinking of the crepe-paper flowers I made to adorn the caskets. We kept a few sprays and wreaths on display, and I sold them to anyone who wanted flowers, as we had no florist shops. They were removed after the services and carried to the cemetery. And in those days everyone stayed until the grave was filled. Then the poor little flowers were placed on the grave, only to be blown down the mountainside by the first gust of wind.

Many strange characters came to the camp. A certain man who was tubercular came to the Victor district hoping the dry air would prove beneficial. When he realized the end was near, he requested that the band should precede him to the cemetery and play "Hot Time in the Old Town Tonight." His request was granted.

CHAPTER XII

VARIOUS PLACES

The business was never the same after the fire. While the building was much nicer and the rooms upstairs were more modern and better furnished, the camp itself was going downhill, and Father began to promote the idea of a little ranch, something more dependable and permanent. He found a nice small place in Cañon City, a comfortable five-room house, and about five acres with bearing apple trees. Of course, he rented a building and sent one of my brothers to carry on the undertaking business in town, until they could dispose of the Victor business and move down on the ranch. Since my husband was in the East on business, I and my five-year-old son Earl moved into the ranch house to look after the cow and a flock of chickens. Having had no experience with chickens, perhaps the care I gave them was not too good. Anyway, they did not produce many eggs, so we decided to kill and dress the ones we thought were nonproducers and ship them to Victor markets. We wanted to do the job right; and since chickens were sold in the markets with head and feet on, that was the way we decided to do it.

My brother Burt was sure he knew how to stick them somewhere in the mouth so they would bleed freely and die immediately. On Saturday we caught what we considered culls and tied them by the feet on the clothes line. He proceeded to stick them. We left them hanging there while we went on an errand. Upon our return we found them tossing wildly about, some of them still able to squawk. They didn't bring quite as much with their heads off, but that was the way it had to be.

It was October and the days were wonderful. The trees were loaded with bright red apples waiting for buyers to come and contract for them on the trees. The ground under the trees was covered with imperfect fruit the wind had blown down. We had a huge wooden barrel, and it was fun to pick up the apples and load them in the light wagon and haul them to the cider mill. It didn't take long to have the barrel full of delicious sweet cider. It also went to Victor to be sold to grocers for Halloween. It arrived when there was a funeral to be held that day, so it was placed on the deck. While the mourners and friends were assembling for the services, my older brother Gil decided he would get a drink of cider. The plug did not come out readily, so he got a hammer and tapped it lightly. It came out. So did the cider. If that plug had struck him in the head it certainly would have killed him. It went right through the ceiling and up into Mother's dining room. The cider went up, then down. It dripped through the floor of the deck onto the people below, and it showered Gil from head to foot. In those days undertakers were dressed up as for a formal affair—black suits with long tails, white shirt with black bow tie, and a tall silk hat. The cider filled the brim of the hat and dripped all over Gil. He was soaked, and a sight. Since he had only one suit and hat, Father had to dress hurriedly in his funeral clothes and conduct the funeral. We never knew what the people thought. They could not have helped hearing the noise, and the smell was so potent that the place reeked like a winery for many weeks. And that barrel of cider was all we ever realized out of that apple crop. A heavy snow came suddenly, then a hard freeze, and the apples were all frozen on the trees.

The following March, Mother and Father moved to the ranch, and later followed me to Salida. Since my husband was a mining promoter, we moved to small camps and they followed for a while, eventually moving to Idaho Falls and going into the undertaking business with my older brother.

That did not prove a success, and they then went to Casper, Wyoming. Casper seemed like a busy mining camp, as oil had been struck and, as usual, in the surrounding areas people were flocking in. My parents liked the excitement, but lacking finances to compete in their line of business, they sought a smaller town in which to start over. Lander was the place. They liked it. They found an old building, and after repairing it and building a deck, they were once more in the furniture business, new and secondhand, and also undertaking. All might have gone well if the store had not burned down. This time they had a little insurance. They bought an old Ford, packed and shipped Mother's best dishes and pictures and a few things of sentimental value—and went back to Victor! This time the deck was divided into two rooms, and that is where they lived.

It was perfectly wonderful what Mother could do with just any place that was livable. That deck took on the most homey look. It was comfortable and clean. The walls were covered with enlarged framed pictures of their parents and our family. When I say the walls were covered, I mean really covered. It looked like an art gallery. My sister Neva called it a rogues' gallery. There were hand-embroidered linens and the cherished Haviland and other beautiful china in her glass cabinet. But it wasn't long until they realized it was a bad move. They had known before they moved back that the camp was not what it had been when they left it. Old friends had either moved away or died, and it was depressing to be constantly reminded of the prosperous, happy boom days, and the reverses that had followed the fire. So it was not too difficult to persuade them to come back to the Springs, where we were now in business, and Father could buy a small interest with us. But he was not so young now. The hours were long, and the work was too heavy for him. We tried to persuade him to take what he could realize for his share, and take life easy with a little financial aid from the children. We should have known better. They did not tell us until the store was all ready to go—a furniture store on the west side, or Old Town, as we called it, where we had first settled when we came from Kansas. Furniture was now cheap, though, and not in demand. Competition was keen, and the store didn't last long.

Just one more unfortunate business venture—a little novelty store in Fountain, a small town near the Springs, and soon they were back in the Springs, and after two more moves, from one little house to another, we finally got them anchored, until five months later Mother died.

Mother was laid to rest just where she said she wanted to live and die, in the shadow of Pikes Peak. Father made his home with us, after sixty-two years of close companionship with Mother, sharing joys and sorrows alike. It was impossible for him to adjust himself to a new life. He often said, "Why couldn't it have been me first? I am afflicted." He was nearly blind and quite deaf. Mother had not worn glasses except to read or sew, and she loved company and took an interest in life.

He lived almost completely in the past. He never tired of telling his interesting experiences to the children and grand-children. Often, as he sat in an easy chair in the sun, he would close his eyes to rest them from the light. I would watch him to see if he was really resting or asleep. Sometimes a smile played on his lips, and often a tear would run slowly down his withered cheek. When we saw the tear, we did not ask him what he was thinking about; but when we saw the smile, and spoke to him, it was always: "Do you remember the time——?" And we would talk and laugh about some humorous experience such as the day of the cider showerbath, or the time he ran away when he was twelve, and how he trudged wearily back the next day.

In the same spirit of adventure with which he had prepared for the many moves earlier, he now anticipated with pleasure the last and permanent move, and the meeting with the numerous loved ones gone on ahead of him. Just as if he was preparing to take a trip, never doubting for an instant that Mother was waiting there for him on that Eternal Deck, where no earthly sorrows or disasters would mar the everlasting joy of their reunion.

CONCLUSION

Life is like a book, made up of chapters; some lives, like mine, of many varied chapters. Others are just a few short stories. Some do not change much, just a continuation of natural, ordinary events, of being born, of living and of dying in small communities or isolated places. Then there are the rovers. Their lives are full of constant changes with no set pattern, and the varied experiences are often exciting.

Looking back over my life, it seems to be made up less perhaps of chapters than of many short stories, each complete. But in each one I am still the leading character. One of the very exciting TV programs, "I Led Three Lives," reminds me somewhat of my own life; only that I never played such important and exciting roles.

The life of the pioneer can be compared to a stroll through a wildwood, destination unknown; perhaps along a narrow path or no path at all—just to wander and discover the many wonders of nature, to rest in the shade of tall trees, or find obstacles to be overcome—a log with tangled branches or vines, or an unexpected stream to block the way, but always the urge to explore and continue to wander.

There was the trip to England to visit my husband's people, whom he had not seen in eighteen years, and the short trip to Liverpool, where we saw Queen Victoria lay the cornerstone for a beautiful cathedral.

With so many completely different chapters, some were bound to be happy and others full of problems and sorrow. In later years my ambitions often meant hard work and worry. For instance, when conditions in our country and my immediate vicinity offered opportunities to make money, one year,

I bought, sold, and rented houses and moved five times. While it was hard work, it also was fun, as the satisfaction of achievement was great, and I had set a goal, not for myself, but for my children's future.

My daughter Betty asked me recently if I knew anyone I would rather be than I, and I could truthfully say I did not. There have been many times I have wished I had unlimited resources, especially at Christmas. One time I had a few hours' lay-over in Chicago, and I spent it in Marshall Field's fabulous store, wishing I could buy for my loved ones any or all of the wonderful things on display. In more recent years, many times, unexpected opportunities for pleasure have presented themselves, like spending an entire day by a tumbling mountain stream, forgetting all the things that should be done at home, thinking only of the beauty around me and the thrill of the sudden strike, and a fish with a bright rainbow down his back, or one with little colorful spots all over him. You sit in the shade of a big pine tree and begrudge the time out for a sandwich; immediately a camp-robber bird and two saucy chipmunks join you to share it. Who could possibly regret such a perfect day?

There was the time I spent two weeks on the beautiful Gunnison River at a fishing lodge known as Richards'. Friends of mine had bought a cabin site and built a small house on it, and since there was no extra room, they put up a tent with cots for me and two small boys. The fishing at that certain time was best at night, and a moonlight night in June is wonderful on the river.

During the day we got our live bait from under the rocks along the bank. They were a tough, slimy black bug called hellgrammites, and were the natural food for trout at that season of the year.

When I came in at night I fastened my hook in the reel and stood it against the tent. During the night the wind blew my rod down and the hook came unfastened. In the dark, I had not taken the bait off the hook, and since those bugs made such good bait—because they stayed on the hook and lived for some time—it was an early breakfast for one of the flock of hens the thrifty owner of the lodge kept to supply boarders with fresh eggs.

We were awakened by a commotion and got up and peered out the flap of the tent. My friend, in his pajamas, was shouting unprintable words and running wildly after a cackling hen, with his little fox terrier barking and in close pursuit. Until all the line was unwound, the hen made pretty good time, but when she had to drag the pole as well, she was slowed down. When they caught her, and quickly cut the line, a very frightened hen ran for home.

While it was really funny, I was anxious to know just what that hen would do, with a hook perhaps caught in her throat, so I made it a point to be present when they were feeding the hens. As far as I could see, they were all eating about the same, and fearing she might have choked or died, I asked how many hens they kept, and for several days I counted them, but none was missing.

I intended to pay for the hen if she came up missing or had trouble with that hook, but I guess that is why chickens have gizzards and can digest everything and anything, even fish-hooks.

Then, too, I think of a very different day, a day at the races, dogs or horses, but preferably horses. The time we went to Tia Juana and had no luck at all, and decided to eni-meni-minie-mo the last race. It fell on Number 1, Argeus, a disreputable-looking long-shot nag. He bucked and finally threw his jockey, and ran all the way back to the paddock. We congratulated ourselves on not having bet on him. But they brought him back with a new jockey, and—you guessed it—he left them all away behind. An old man standing by me at the rail, who had re-gretted having a ticket on Number 1, showed me his ticket and asked if he had won. Later, we found him huddled on the steps, really worried about his four hundred dollars, because he was an old-age pensioner.

Then the time we had bets on win and place, near the end of the last stretch and—tragedy or tragedies—one tripped the other. They shot one right there, and carried our last hope away on a stretcher.

The wise little ants and squirrels store only what is good for the long winter ahead. If out of the abundance of good we gather along the way, we were as wise as they, and picked and stored only the memories of the blessings and pleasures of life, there would be little or no room for unpleasant and un-happy thoughts to enter.

Memories like these will soon flock around my old rocking chair along with some that are sad, since of the family of ten children I am the last; but the old rocking chair will have other joys and interests as my children, grandchildren and great-grand-children gather around and beg for a story "of the old days," and out of my store of memories I may find one to please each one. At least it will be the means of keeping them coming to visit me.

While I do not have a deep pocket with an endless supply of peppermint candies and nickels, I do have a never-ending supply of stories they love to hear.